LOCKHEED F-117 NIGHTHAWKS

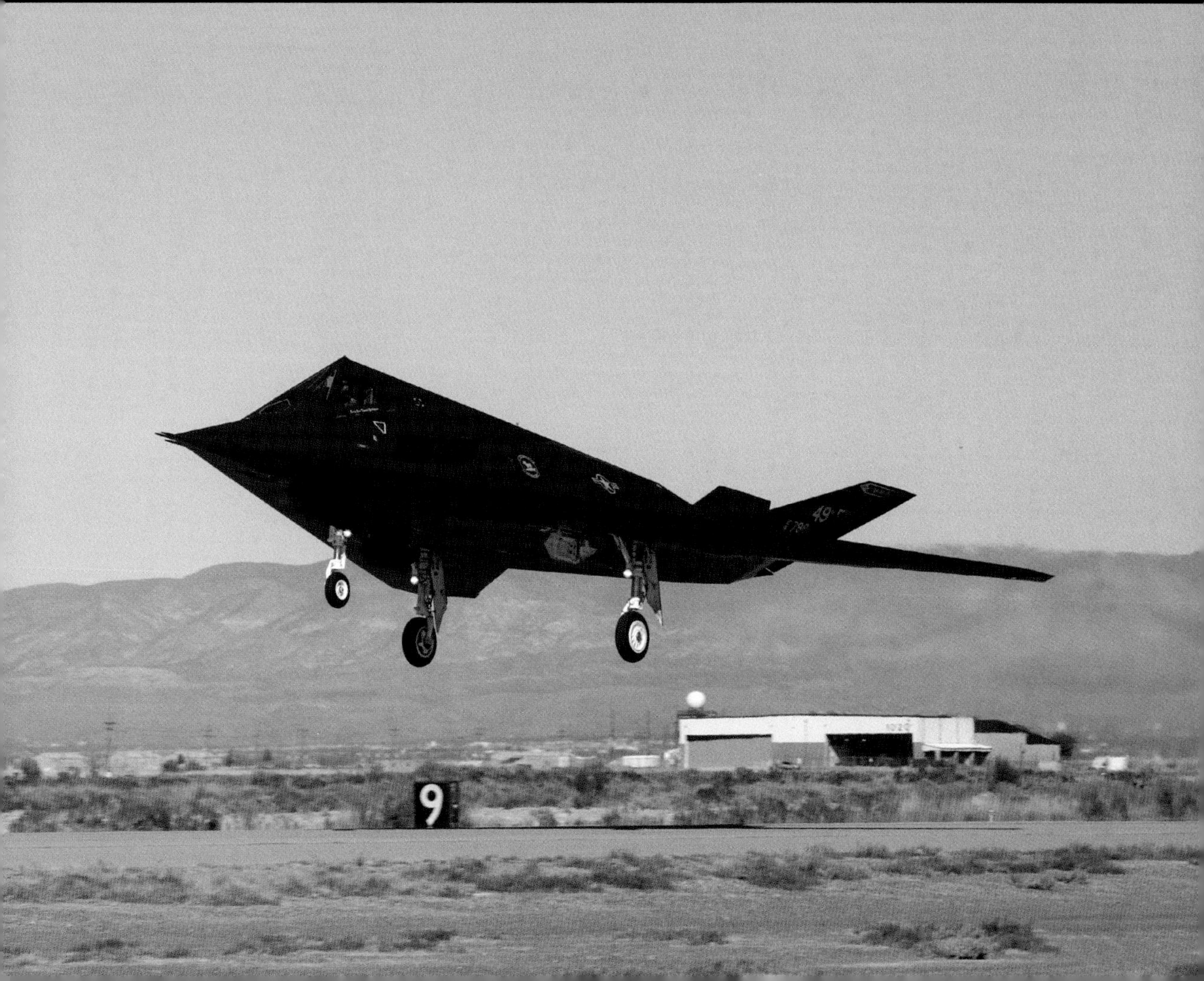

(Don Logan Photo)

LOCKHEED F-117 NIGHT HAWKS

A Stealth Fighter Roll Call

Don Logan

Schiffer Military History
Atglen, PA

ACKNOWLEDGEMENTS

I would like to thank the Operations Personnel and the Public Affairs Office of the 49th Fighter Wing Holloman AFB, the USAF Weapons School, Kevin Helm, Denny Lombard of Lockheed Martin, Tony Landis, Greg Meland, and Brian C. Rogers without whose help I could not have put this book together.

I would also like to thank the following individuals who provided photographs included in this book: David F. Brown, Richard Cooper, Damon J. Duran, Matt Ellis, Peter Greengrass, Jerry Geer, Norris Graser, Tim Hunter, Jim Haseltine, Marty Isham, Kevin Jackson, Tom Kaminski, Craig Kaston, Ben Knowles, Bob Leavitt, Nate Leong, Frank McCurdy, David Menard, Stan Piet, Gerhard Plomitzer, Brian C. Rogers, Mick Roth, Pete Snowdon, Keith Snyder, Norman E. Taylor, Randy Walker, and Dr. Séan Wilson. F-117 art side views were drawn by Jack Morris JDMC Aviation Graphics.

Book design by Robert Biondi and Don Logan.

Printed in China.
ISBN: 978-0-7643-3242-5

We are always looking for people to write books on new and related subjects. If you have an idea for a book, please contact us at the address below.

Published by Schiffer Publishing Ltd. 4880 Lower Valley Road Atglen, PA 19310 Phone: (610) 593-1777 FAX: (610) 593-2002 E-mail: Info@schifferbooks.com. Visit our web site at: www.schifferbooks.com Please write for a free catalog. This book may be purchased from the publisher. Please include $5.00 postage. Try your bookstore first.	In Europe, Schiffer books are distributed by: Bushwood Books 6 Marksbury Ave. Kew Gardens, Surrey TW9 4JF England Phone: 44 (0)20 8392-8585 FAX: 44 (0)20 8392-9876 E-mail: info@bushwoodbooks.co.uk www.bushwoodbooks.co.uk Free postage in the UK. Europe: air mail at cost. Try your bookstore first.

Contents

88-0843 goes vertical during a flight in March 2008. (Richard Cooper Photo)

Introduction

This pictorial book is a history of the F-117 Night Hawk Stealth Fighter. However, it does not attempt to cover an in-depth history of the Stealth Fighter program or the people involved; instead it is a "Roll Call" of the F-117 with individual history and photos of each F-117. In addition the book includes a short program history, operating locations and Air Force bases, production sites associated with the F-117; F-117 Units, F-117 aircraft, and Information and photos of the A-7 and T-38 aircraft used to support the F-117 program. Though the photos cover the full history of the F-117 program, many of the photos were taken in the last two years at bases including Holloman AFB, Nellis AFB, and Edwards AFB.

(Don Logan Photo)

(Don Logan Photo)

F-117 History

Project Harvey

In 1975, Ed Martin and Ben Rich solicited the help of five engineers from Lockheed's Advanced Design and Skunk Works Engineers to help prepare a proposal for the Experimental Survivable Testbed (XST) program using discretionary funds. This Lockheed XST Program was named "Project Harvey" after the 1950 movie titled *Harvey*, starring James Stewart, about an invisible six-foot rabbit that could only be seen by one person, Stewart. The product of Project Harvey was the Hopeless Diamond.

Hopeless Diamond

During 1975, Skunk Work engineers began working on an aircraft which would have a greatly reduced radar cross section that would make it all but invisible to enemy radars, but would nevertheless still be able to fly and carry out its combat mission. The technique that they came up with was known as faceting, in which the ordinarily smooth surface of the airframe is broken up into a series of trapezoidal or triangular flat surfaces. The surfaces were arranged in such a way that the vast majority of the radar incident on the aircraft will be scattered away from the aircraft at odd angles, leaving very little to be reflected directly back into the receiver. An additional reduction in radar cross section was to be obtained by covering the entire surface of the aircraft with radar absorbent material (RAM). One of the disadvantages involved in the use of faceting on aerodynamic surfaces was that it tended to produce an aircraft which was inherently unstable about all three axes – pitch, roll, and yaw.

(Kevin Jackson Photo)

9

The airframe design was a flyable, controllable aircraft with no curved surfaces at all, except for small-radius, straight edges to its wings and tail surfaces. It was as if a diamond had been cut to the shape of an aircraft, and the technique came to be called "faceting". Using a Cray computer, a program was developed that could model the scattering from the new faceted shapes, and predict their Radar Cross Section (RCS), in a reasonable amount of time.

Because this early work was totally funded with Lockheed funds, the computer program and the faceted designs belonged to Lockheed. Lockheed owns the patent for the faceted designs. From the computer program, the Skunk Works engineers created a ten-foot wooden model dubbed the "Hopeless Diamond". The model was taken to an outdoor radar test range on the Mojave Desert near Palmdale. The model was mounted on a twelve-foot high pole, and the radar dish zeroed in from about 1,500 feet away. The site radar operator could not see the model on the radar, until a black bird landed right on top of the Hopeless Diamond. The radar was only picking up the bird.

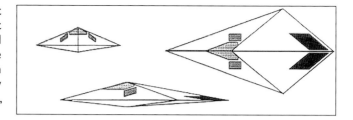

In March 1976, the Skunk Works built a model out of wood, all flat panels, thirty-eight feet long, and painted black. It was hauled to White Sands New Mexico for competition against Northrop's candidate. The Skunk Works model had a lower RCS than the pole it was mounted on so Lockheed built a new pole. In April 1976, Lockheed won the competition and the "Have Blue" program was born. Lockheed was the winner, not only because the Hopeless Diamond's low RCS, but also because Lockheed had a computer model which could predict the signature – something that the competition did not have.

HAVE BLUE Pole model on the RCS test range at White Sands, New Mexico. (Lockheed Martin Aeronautics Company)

Have Blue

The F-117A was the first warplane to be specifically designed from the outset for low radar observability. Lockheed Advanced Development Projects (better known as the "Skunk Works") began working on stealth as far back as the late 1950s, and low radar observability had played a role in the design of the A-12/YF-12/SR-71 series of Mach 3+ aircraft.

In early 1977, Lockheed received a contract from the Defense Advanced Research Projects Agency (DARPA) for the construction of two sixty-percent scale flyable test aircraft under a project named Have Blue. The name Have Blue seems to have no specific meaning, probably having been chosen at random from an approved list of secret project names. Many of USAF's acquisition programs and projects, particularly those that were classified or otherwise sensitive, were assigned two-word designations starting with Have or Senior. Shortly after the Have Blue contract was let, the project was transferred over to Air Force System Command control and became highly "black" – in other words, a special access program, with all information about it being highly classified and restricted to those with a need to know. Outside of a few people at Lockheed and the Defense Department, no one knew that Have Blue even existed.

The two Have Blue aircraft were built at Lockheed in only a few months. The first aircraft was intended to evaluate the type's flying characteristics, whereas the second was to evaluate the radar signature. In order to save some time and money, existing off-the-shelf components were used where feasible. The engines were a pair of standard production non-afterburning General Electric J85s from the U.S. Navy North American T-2B Buckeye. They were mounted in enclosures sitting atop the wings. The main landing gear was taken from a Fairchild Republic A-10, and fly-by-wire components were scavenged from an F-16. The instrumentation and the ejection seat were taken from a Northrop F-5. The Have Blue aircraft had the same general shape as that which would later become familiar with the F-117A, except that the twin rudders were located forward of the exhaust ejectors and were angled inward rather than outward. The inward cant was about thirty degrees.

The leading edge of the semi-delta wing was swept back at 72.5 degrees. The wing featured two inboard trailing edge elevons for pitch and roll control. Four spoilers (two on top of the wing and two on the bottom) were mounted just forward of the elevons. There were no flaps or speed brakes. The wing trailing edge was less deeply notched than that of the F-117A. A single cockpit with an ejection seat was provided. The Have Blue aircraft employed V-type windshields (similar to those of the F-102/F-106). No weapons bay or any sort of tactical equipment was fitted.

The Have Blue aircraft were equipped with fly-by-wire (FBW) flight controls that were adapted from the F-16 system. However, the system had to be modified to handle an aircraft that was unstable about all three axes (the F-16 is unstable only about the pitch axis). The problem of designing a stealthy system for airspeed measurement had not yet been solved, and the aircraft were equipped with a conventional pitot tube that retracted when they were being tested for radar reflections. The inertial navigation system provided enough speed data for test purposes when the probe was retracted.

Two prototypes were built at a cost of $37 million for both aircraft. Lockheed workers assembled the two Have Blue aircraft in a cordoned-off area in Building 83C, Burbank, California. Neither aircraft ever received an official DoD designation, nor did they get a USAF serial number. However, Lockheed did give the aircraft its own manufacturer's serial numbers, 1001 and 1002.

The first example (1001) was finished in November of 1977. In order to keep the project away from prying eyes, the Have Blue prototype was shipped out to the Groom Lake Test Facility in Nevada in high secrecy for the test flights. Groom Lake is located in a particularly remote area of the Nellis test range complex, and is a good location for the testing of secret aircraft. A camouflage paint scheme was applied to make it hard for unwanted observers at Groom Lake to determine the aircraft's shape.

The first flight of the Have Blue took place in January or February of 1978, with veteran Lockheed test pilot William M. "Bill" Park at the controls. At an early stage Lt.Col. Norman Kenneth "Ken" Dyson of the USAF assisted Park in the flight test program.

Flight test of the Have Blue initially went fairly smoothly, and the fly-by-wire system functioned well. The landing speed was quite high (160 knots), as expected because of the lack of flaps or speed brakes. However, on May 4, 1978, Have Blue prototype number 1001 was landing after a routine test flight when it hit the ground excessively hard, jamming the right main landing gear in a semi-retracted position. Pilot Bill Park pulled the aircraft back into the air, and repeatedly tried to shake the gear back down again. After his third attempt failed, he was ordered to take the aircraft up to 10,000 feet and eject. Park ejected successfully, but he hit his head and was knocked unconscious. Since he was unable to control his parachute during descent or landing, his back was severely injured on impact. He survived, but was forced to retire from flying. The Have Blue aircraft was destroyed in the crash.

Have Blue 1002 arrived at Groom Lake shortly after the loss of number 1. It took to the air for the first time in June of 1978, with Lt.Col. Ken Dyson at the controls. From mid-1978 until early 1979, Dyson flew more than sixty-five test sorties, testing the response of the aircraft to various types of radar threats. The Have Blue prototype 1002 proved to be essentially undetectable by all airborne radars except the Boeing E-3 AWACS, which could only acquire the aircraft at short ranges. Most ground-based missile tracking radars could detect the Have Blue only after it was well inside the minimum range for the surface-to-air missiles with which they were associated. Neither ground-based radars nor air-to-air missile guidance radars could lock onto the aircraft. It was found that the best tactic to avoid radar detection was to approach the radar site head on, presenting the Have Blue's small nose-on signature.

Application of the RAM proved to be rather tricky, and ground crews had to be careful to seal all joints thoroughly before each flight. RAM came in linoleum-like sheets, which were cut to shape and bonded to the skin to cover large areas. Doors and access panels had to be carefully checked and adjusted for a tight fit between flights and all gaps had to be filled with conductive tape and then covered with RAM. Paint-type RAM was available, but it had to be built up by hand, coat by coat. Even the gaps around the canopy and the fuel-filler door had to be filled with paint-type RAM before each flight. Ground crews had to make sure that all surface screws were completely tight, since even one loose screw for an access panel could make the aircraft show up during radar signature tests.

Have Blue number 1002 was lost in July of 1979. During its fifty-second flight, with Lt.Col. Dyson at the controls, one of its J85 engines caught fire. The subsequent fire was so intense that the hydraulic fluid lines were burned through. Lt.Col. Dyson was forced to eject, and 1002 was a total loss. No further Have Blue aircraft were built, since the general concept had been proven.

F-117

The gain of valuable engineering data during the Have Blue flight test program led to a Full Scale Development (FSD) decision by the Air Force and contract award to the Lockheed Skunk Works on November 16, 1978. The original order was for five FSD test aircraft and fifteen production articles. The initial F-117 delivered in June 1981 and subsequent production lots of varying quantities yielded a total of sixty-four aircraft built through July 1990. As of May 2001, fifty-one production and three FSD test aircraft were still active.

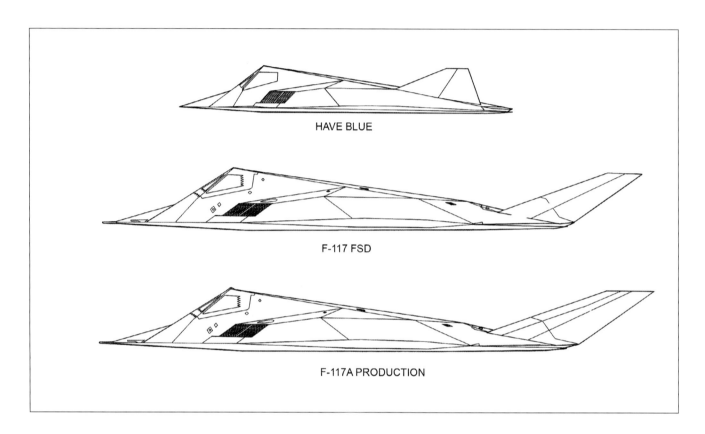

HAVE BLUE

F-117 FSD

F-117A PRODUCTION

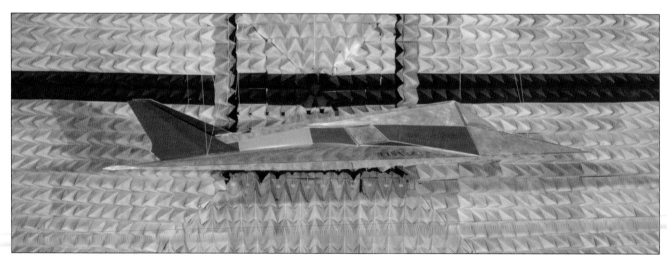

A radar cross section model of the Have Blue aircraft in Lockheed's anechoic test facility. (Lockheed Martin Aeronautics Company)

Streamlined management by Aeronautical Systems Center, Wright-Patterson AFB, Ohio, in close coordination with the Skunk Works, combined breakthrough stealth technology with concurrent development and production. The result of this effort, shrouded in secrecy rivaling that of the Manhattan Project to develop the atomic bomb, was declaration of Initial Operating Capability (IOC) after delivery of the fourteenth F-117 in October 1983. Incredibly, IOC occurred in just under five years after production go ahead, about half the time for most programs.

An F-117 on the assembly line at Lockheed's Burbank, California facility. (Lockheed Martin Aeronautics Company)

Plywood mock-up of the F-117 at Lockheed's Burbank, California facility. (Lockheed Martin Aeronautics Company)

F-117 Operations

4450th Tactical Group – Tonopah Test Range Air Field

Beginning in 1982, the 4450th Tactical Group operated the F-117 the first years of its existence at the Tonopah Test Range. This covert facility in central Nevada at the north end of the Nellis complex, enabled the concurrent development and production of the F-117 to continue far from the prying eyes of the media. The 4450th Tactical Group was never a test organization. The designation "4450th Tactical Group" was an attempt to disguise the fact that there was a "Wing" sized organization operating covertly at Nellis AFB. The cover story for the 4450th was that they were testing avionics using the A-7, but it was never an actual test organization. The 4450th and its follow-on organization the 37th TFW were combat ready from the day that IOC was declared. By late 1989, as the F-117 was reaching maturity and now a publicly acknowledged program, the Air Force wanted to redefine its operating command to a combat unit. In October 1989, the 4450th was inactivated and the program reorganized as the 37th Tactical Fighter Wing, which continued to operate the F-117 through its first combat employments.

37th Fighter Wing – Tonopah Test Range, Nevada

The 37th Tactical Fighter Wing was redesignated 37th Fighter Wing on 1 October 1991, replacing the 37th TFW with no change in commander, personnel or equipment. When the USAF decided to move the F-117 force to Holloman AFB, New Mexico, partly to reduce operating costs now that the

secrecy of Tonopah was no longer needed, a decision was made to preserve the identity of the 49th Fighter Wing, which was then at Holloman (but giving up its F-15 Eagle fleet), and to retire the 37th designation. With the shift to Holloman, the F-117 operational wing became the 49th Fighter Wing on 5 July 1992.

49th Fighter Wing Holloman AFB, New Mexico

Coming out of the "Black World" following the successful Desert Storm campaign, the F117's transition to conventional operations at a relatively open site was a natural progression to fully integrate the F-117 into the Air Force arsenal. Such a move would also yield substantial cost savings, as the USAF would no longer need to employ a small charter airline to shuttle program personnel between Nellis and Tonopah, could eliminate the extensive – and expensive – security measures associated with keeping the program "black," and could mothball the Tonopah base, which was expensive to operate by virtue of its remoteness. By mid-1992, the F-117 Wing transferred operations to Holloman Air Force Base at Alamogordo, New Mexico. At the same time the program moved to the 49th Fighter Wing, which carried on the proud heritage of forty-three air aces from the Second World War. The F-117 continued operations from Holloman AFB; flying combat missions over Iraq from Ahmed al-Jaber Air Base in Kuwait for Operations Southern Watch/Provide Comfort, flying combat missions over Kosovo from Aviano Air Base, Italy during Operation Allied Force, and flying combat over Iraq from Al Udeid Air Base in Qatar during Operation Iraqi

Brigadier General David Goldfein, 49 FW Commander in 81-10795 writes down some final information prior to departure of the first group of F-117 from Holloman. (USAF)

Freedom. Retirement of the F-117 began on 13 March 2007 when the first seven of the 49th Fighter Wing's F-117s left for storage in their original hangars back at the airfield at Tonopah Test Range.

Over the next thirteen months the F-117 left Holloman in a total of seven groups culminating with the last four aircraft departing on 21 April 2008. Test and Test support F-117 operations continued with the 410th Flight Test Squadron at Palmdale, California until the 410th's inactivation on 1 August 2008.

Above: The first group of F-117 to be retired lined up on the Holloman ramp on 13 March 2007 prior to departure. 80-0789, 80-0790, 81-10795, 85-0817, 85-0832, and the Gray Dragon 85-0835 were the first six jets to be retired. (USAF) Below: The first group of retired F-117s inside a hangar at Tonopah.

The Last F-117 produced 88-0843 leads the last retirement flight from Holloman down initial at Palmdale California on 22 April 2008. The other three aircraft are 86-0824, 84-0809, and 84-0800. (Damon J. Duran Photo)

A takeoff into the setting sun at Holloman AFB on 15 October 2007. (Dr. Séan Wilson Prime Images Photo)

Marked as the 49th FW Flagship aircraft 2005-4088 was the first of two F-22s which arrived at Holloman on 2 June 2008. (USAF)

Marked as the 7th FS Flagship aircraft 2005-4106 was the wingman of 4088 on 2 June 2008. Both F-22s had been previously assigned to the 1st FW at Langley AFB, Virginia. (USAF)

A four ship over the Nellis ranges on 12 February 2007. (Dr. Séan Wilson Prime Images Photo)

F-117 Units and Organizations

F-117 OPERATIONAL UNITS

Baja Scorpions

The name Baja Scorpions was conceived very early in the F-117 Flight Test Program. The F-117 Flight Test group was located in a complex at the south end of the Groom Lake, Nevada test site. To the rest of the personnel at the test site, they were known as the South Enders. From this was derived Baja, the Spanish word (loosely translated) for south. A rattlesnake first came to mind when searching for a mascot. However, this was decided against because, unlike the radar-eluding F-117, the rattlesnake provides ample warning prior to striking. Then, one day, a scorpion was found in one of the hangars and captured. Because scorpions strike without warning, this potentially dangerous creature turned out to be a blessing by providing a symbolic mascot.

4450th Tactical Group

The 4450th TG was activated on 15 October 1979. The four-digit number signifies a major command-controlled organization group not entitled to permanent military lineage or heraldry. The best-kept secret of the time was the development of a strike aircraft intended to be largely invisible to radar, and the 4450th – also known as the A-Unit, one of a series of designations devised for everyday use because they conveyed no meaning – began life at Nellis AFB, Nevada, awaiting the mystery aircraft. The group began rotating pilots and maintenance personnel through the super-secret Groom Lake, Nevada, facility in 1981, although the group's home was always meant to be the Tonopah Test Range (TTR) airfield, also in Nevada.

All the units in the 4450th TG were assigned a squadron number that was classified and an alphabetical unit designator that was used for everyday identification of the unit. The reasoning behind this was so that someone outside the program would not be able to determine the size of the 4450th TG.

By using the normal squadron designations (i.e. 4451st Test Squadron, 4452nd Test Squadron, etc) someone could eventually estimate the size of the group based on the number of squadrons they heard about. By using alphabetic designators

(I Unit, Q Unit, etc) it was thought that no one could figure out the size of the organization. The group's Detachment 1, alias the Q-Unit set up shop at Tonopah. Initially housed in mobile homes once operated by a Chevron oil-drilling site, it was soon followed by the group headquarters. The group's Detachment 2, or R-Unit, activated with the group on 15 October 1979 and was a small flight-test detachment which apparently kept a handful of test pilots at Burbank (later Palmdale) and Groom Lake.

The pilots in Det. 2 (R Unit) were not "kept" at Burbank. They were the FOLLOW-ON OPERATIONAL TEST & EVALUATION (FOT&E) pilots and worked at the classified site known to those in the program as PS22 (which stood for Project Site 22). Presumably PS22 was at Groom Lake, but it was never acknowledged. When required, the Det. 2 pilots would fly to Burbank to consult with Lockheed engineers, but no flying occurred at Lockheed's Burbank facility.

By September 1982 Detachment 1, with the first operational pilots who flew the Senior Trend F-117 aircraft, evolved into 4452nd Test Squadron "Goat Suckers", still called the Q-Unit. The first squadrons in the group, however, were the 4450th Test Squadron (I-Unit) and 4451st Test Squadron (P-Unit) and were activated on 11 June 1981. The P-Unit operated the Vought A-7D aircraft stationed at Nellis AFB, Nevada, which served at first to give pilots flying time and to cover their true purpose; once F-117s began to enter service the A-7Ds were used as chase, or companion, aircraft.

The 4450th Tactical Group accepted the first operational F-117 (80-0787) at Tonopah on 23 August 1982, after the aircraft had passed initial trials at Groom Lake. The group attained IOC (initial operating capability) on 28 October 1983 with delivery of its fourteenth aircraft. The group's third squadron, filling out its intended strength from the beginning, was the 4453rd Test and Evaluation Squadron "Grim Reaper", or the Z-Unit, activated on 1 October 1985.

4450th Test Squadron (I-Unit) Nightstalkers

The 4450th Test Squadron (TS) was one of two squadrons (with the 4451st TS) activated under the 4450th TG on 11 June 1981, some fourteen months before the first operational Senior Trend F-117 aircraft was delivered. The Nightstalkers flew F-117 aircraft from late 1982 onwards. The squadron was inactivated 5 October 1989. On that date, the squadron's people and equipment remained at Tonopah and the Nightstalkers were reorganized as the 415th Tactical Fighter Squadron.

4451st Test Squadron (P-Unit), Nellis AFB, Nevada (later Tonopah)

The 4451st TS was activated on 15 January 1983. The 4451st Test Squadron (P-Unit) operated Vought A-7D/K aircraft at Nellis. The unit flew the A-7 as a chase aircraft and an aircraft that the pilots could fly to maintain some proficiency. It wasn't a "full sized" squadron in the normal sense of a fighter squadron. It had a handful of personnel assigned. Most of the pilots were assigned to the other squadrons and they borrowed the A-7s when they needed to fly chase or do proficiency flying. The 4451st was never equipped with F-117s. The P-Unit was inactivated on 5 October 1989. On that same day, the 417 TFTS (Tactical Fighter Training Squadron) was activated and assumed the mission of the 4451st TESTS (P-Unit). When the A-7s were retired in 1989, the 417th TFTS was given a handful of T-38s to fly chase for the F-117 training missions.

4452nd Test Squadron (Q-Unit) Goat Suckers

The 4452nd TS "Goat Suckers" (Q-Unit) began as Detachment 1 of the 4450th and was assigned to Tonopah during the brief period when group headquarters remained at Nellis. The Goat Suckers took on the popular term for the American Night Hawk, even though Lockheed never succeeded in persuading the USAF to adopt Nighthawk as the nickname for the F-117 aircraft. The 4452nd TESTS, while designated a squadron with a number, was the test unit that flew the first four pre-production F-117s for various tests as part of the concurrent development/production contract with Lockheed. In 1988 it was also given a production aircraft for use in developmental testing bringing its total aircraft complement to five. It was never a full strength squadron. The squadron was inactivated on 30 May 1989, becoming the only stealth unit not to acquire a new identity as part of the 37th TFW later in the year.

Dragon Test Team (R-Unit)

The R-Unit was the Follow-on Operational Test & Evaluation (FOT&E) unit that was called the Dragon Test Team and became the detachment that was transferred from the Det. 1, 57th TFW down to Det. 1, 53rd TEG.

4453rd Test and Evaluation Squadron (Z-Unit) Grim Reapers

The 4453rd Test and Evaluation Squadron Grim Reaper (Z-Unit) was activated on 1 October 1985 to become the second F-117 operational (combat) squadron to fly the F-117 in the 4450th Tactical Group. Their primary combat orientation was the Pacific theater in the event that they were ever to actually be deployed. The squadron was inactivated on 5 October 1989, when its people and equipment, remaining in place at Tonopah, became the 416th Tactical Fighter Squadron.

Below: F-117 hangar at Tonopah in 1991. (Lockheed Martin Aeronautics Company)

37TH TACTICAL FIGHTER WING

When the F-117 was made public, the USAF no longer needed a provisional group to operate the aircraft. Furthermore, the identity of a line fighter wing, the 37th TFW (which was then winding down F-4G Advanced Wild Weasel operations at George AFB, California) was available for immediate transfer. On 5 October 1989, the USAF inactivated the 4450th TG and put the 4450th people and equipment under the 37th TFW banner. In practical terms, this was a change of name only, as everything stayed in place and Tonopah remained the home of the 37th Tactical Fighter Wing.

The 37th TFW emblem at George AFB had been a simpler emblem. During its activation in the 1940s, the 37th group used a simple emblem – the Air Force yellow cross on an Air Force blue shield – that signified its history as the "Defender of the Crossroads" which referred to the 37th Pursuit Group's defense of the Panama Canal Zone during World War II. The group's emblem then differed slightly from its emblem today, after becoming an F-117 unit the Nighthawk from the 4450th emblem was added to the previous 37th TFW emblem.

The 37th Tactical Fighter Wing took over the three F-117 groups' squadrons that were redesignated 415th TFS (former 4450th TS), 416th TFS (former 4453rd TES) and 417th TFTS (former 4451st TS).

In December 1989, for Operation Just Cause, the 37th TFW launched eight aircraft from Tonopah Test Range. Two of those aircraft were "air spares" and accompanied the primary aircraft for a good portion of the trip across the U.S. The other six aircraft went all the way to Panama. The pilots were in communication with the Army command post (or whoever was directing the battle) and only two aircraft were directed to drop their bombs. After they completed their mission, the F-117s flew on to England AFB and landed after being airborne for approximately 14 hours. All six aircraft landed code-1 (no maintenance problems to fix). Upon landing at England, the F-117s were promptly stuffed away inside hangars normally used for fuel system maintenance at England and were launched the next night back to Tonopah.

The 37th TFW deployed for Operation Desert Shield and flew combat in Desert Storm. The Wing deployed its 415th TFS to the Persian Gulf region in August 1990 and its 416th TFS in December 1990; its third flying squadron, the 417th TFTS, remained at home at Tonopah but provided personnel and aircraft for the build-up against Iraq.

The deployed 37th TFW was designated a provisional wing on 20 December 1990 to bring its nomenclature in line with other wings preparing at that time for a possible war with Iraq. The 37th TFW (P) designation was applicable to the bulk of the F-117 wing when it was deployed to King Khalid Air Base, Khamis Mushait, Saudi Arabia.

On 17 January 1991 six F-117 aircraft and a small group of maintenance personnel were deployed from Tonopah to Langley AFB. These aircraft were being pre-positioned as attrition aircraft. They sat at Langley for a week or so and were finally deployed to Saudi Arabia to join the rest of the F-117 fleet.

Original 37th Tactical Fighter Wing Emblem

Night Hawk 37th Tactical Fighter Wing Emblem

The war began on 17 January 1991 and ended forty days later. The U.S. Air Force later said that the 37th TFW's F-117s comprised only 2.5 per cent of the shooters in-theater on the first day of the war against Iraq, yet credited them with hitting over thirty-one percent of the targets. The unit's provisional designation was dropped after the war and most of the 37th TFW returned to Tonopah, but the wing left some aircraft at Khamis Mushait as a contingency and to retain a striking potential in support of Operation Southern Watch, the coalition's enforcement of a No-Fly Zone in Kurdish areas of northern Iraq. This Middle East presence has involved periodic rotation of squadrons and personnel.

415th Tactical Fighter Squadron Nightstalkers

The 415th Tactical Fighter Squadron came into existence on 5 October 1989 with the people and equipment of the former 4450th TS. The 415th TFS provided some of the pilots who flew 416th TFS F-117s on the 19 December 1989 combat mission to Panama during Operation Just Cause.

Under contingency plans of the late 1980s, the squadron was considered to be the Atlantic component of the stealth fighter community, expected to support the USAF Europe in time of war. In fact, when war came in the Middle East, the squadron supported U.S. Central Command during Operation Desert Shield.

The Nightstalkers were the first of the Wing's squadrons to be deployed to Khamis Mushait, Saudi Arabia, in Desert Shield. The 415th deployed to Saudi Arabia on August 19, 1990 with a stop at Langley AFB.

The squadron bore the brunt of the difficult build-up in the Middle East, bolstered by a few personnel and aircraft from the 416th TFS (which deployed in December 1990) and 417th TFTS (which remained stateside but provided aircraft and personnel). The Nightstalkers fought in Operation Desert Storm from the first night, 17 January 1991, until the end on 26 February 1991, The 415th TFS had the first F-117 contingent to return from the Gulf War, eight aircraft which landed at Nellis AFB on 1 April 1991.

In keeping with USAF reorganization policies, the 415th TFS became the 415th FS on 1 November 1991. Another change in USAF nomenclature put an end to emblems and nicknames with satanic connotations, no matter obscure: with this change in late 1992 the Nightstalkers lost their proud nickname and became, instead, the Nighthawks.

When the F-117 force moved from Tonopah to Holloman AFB, New Mexico on 5 July 1992, the 37th FW became the 49th FW, but the squadron designation was not, at first, changed. For a time, 415th FS could not take on the name of the 9th Fighter Squadron because that designator was employed (from May 1992) by the F-4E Phantom unit which trains German Luftwaffe pilots; on 30 July 1993 the Phantom unit reverted to its earlier designator as the 20th FS, a move which enabled the 415th FS, in turn, to be reorganized as the 9th Fighter Squadron on that date.

416th Tactical Fighter Squadron Ghostriders

The 416th Tactical Fighter Squadron came into existence on 5 October 1989 with the people and equipment of the former 4453rd Test and Evaluation Squadron.

The Pacific component of the 37th TFW earmarked for U.S. Pacific Command (meaning Korea) in the event of war, the Ghostriders were not at first chosen for deployment when Operation Desert Storm began in August 1990. As the build-up in the Middle East grew, the decision was made to deploy the squadron, and the long trip to Khamis Mushait, Saudi Arabia (with a stopover at Langley AFB, Virginia) began on 2 December 1990. The Ghostriders fought in Operation Desert Storm from the first night, 17 January 1991, until the end in the early morning hours of 28 February 1991. In the immediate post-Desert Storm era, the 416th TFS made a deployment to Korea where it was part of contingency plans for a conflict there.

In keeping with USAF reorganization, the 416th TFS lost its tactical nomenclature and was redesignated 416th Fighter Squadron on 1 November 1991.

When the F-117 force moved from Tonopah to Holloman AFB, New Mexico, on 5 July 1992, the parent 37th FW relinquished its designation in order to adopt the colors and lineage of the 49th FW. Squadron designations, however, were not changed at first. The Ghostriders inactivated on 30 July 1993, and its personnel and equipment took on the identity of the 8th Fighter Squadron "Black Sheep."

417th Tactical Fighter Training Squadron Bandits

The 417th TFTS was formed on 5 October 1989 from the assets of the 4451st Test Squadron, the Bandits. The squadron served as the FTU (formal training unit) for the F-117 and took over operation of the stealth community's Northrop T-38 Talon chase aircraft.

The 417th TFTS did not deploy during Operations Desert Shield/Storm but provided six aircraft to stand by at Langley AFB, Virginia, as attrition replacements for the F-117 force in the Middle East. In the event, there was no attrition and the aircraft were not needed. The 417th TFTS was redesignated 417th Fighter Squadron on 1 November 1991.

When the F-117 force moved to Holloman AFB, the 417th FS was the last of the three F-117 squadrons to assume a new identity traditionally associated with its parent wing. Equipped with ten F-117s and eleven AT-38B Talons, the squadron was inactivated and replaced by the 7th Fighter Squadron on 1 December 1993. Later, the 417th was again activated at Holloman flying 49th FW F-117s on 13 August 2003 as the 417th Weapons Squadron (WPS), a Geographically Separated Unit (GSU) of the USAF Weapons School at Nellis AFB, Nevada. The 417th was again inactivated on 15 September 2006 after graduating its last class of F-117 Weapons Officers.

49TH FIGHTER WING (HO), HOLLOMAN AFB, NEW MEXICO

The 49th Fighter Wing took over the F-117 squadrons and the equipment and personnel of the dismantled 37th Fighter Wing when the move from Tonopah to Holloman AFB, New Mexico, was made on 5 July 1992.

The USAF simply could not dispense with the identity of the 49th FW, which had a proud history dating to 15 January 1941 when the 49th Pursuit Group (Interceptor) trained in Seversky P-35s before moving to New Guinea. Among its forty-three air aces were Lieutenant Colonel Boyd D. Buzz Wagner, the first American ace in the Pacific theatre, and Major Richard I. Bong, who scored forty aerial victories. The 49th fought in Korea with F-80s and F-84s, flew F-4 Phantoms in Southeast Asia and during the Cold War, and operated F-15 Eagles immediately prior to the change to F-117s.

When it received its F-117s, the 49th FW took on the three flying squadrons, namely the 415th Fighter Squadron Nighthawks (formerly Nightstalkers), which was redesignated as 9th Fighter Squadron on 30 July 1993; the 416th Fighter Squadron Ghostriders, redesignated 8th Fighter Squadron on 30 July 1993; and the 417th Fighter Squadron Bandits, redesignated 7th Fighter Squadron in December 1993. The last-named squadron change had to await the transfer of the wing's IFF (introduction to fighter fundamentals) training, performed in the AT-38B Talon, to Air Education and Training Command.

The move to Holloman brought the Cockroach, or Black Jet, out into the open, both literally and figuratively. While many aspects of F-117 operations remained classified, the warplane was no longer part of a black program.

Eighteen F-117s lined up in the "Canyon" between the hangars at Holloman AFB. (USAF)

7th Fighter Squadron Bunyaps/Screamin Demons

The 7th Fighter Squadron Bunyaps took over the F-117 operations of the former 417th FS Bandits in December 1993. The Bunyaps got their nickname from a mythical fanged creature in the lore of Australian Aborigines and owe their origins to the 7th Pursuit Squadron (Interceptor) formed on 20 November 1940 with Seversky P-35s. Curiously, the devil-like creature in the Bunyaps emblem (approved in 1944) has survived the USAF's ban on satanic images even though the Nightstalkers and Ghostriders of the recent past did not, The squadron's history includes combat in New Guinea and the Philippines in P-40s, P-47s and P-38s; in Korea in F-80s and F-84s; and Cold War flying in the F-100, F-105, F-4 and F-15. Just before becoming an F-117 operator, the squadron performed IFF (introduction to fighter fundamentals) training for future fighter pilots using the AT-38B Talon. The time consumed in winding down and transferring this function meant that the 8th and 9th FS became F-117 operators fully nine months before the 7th FS did. The 7th FS was now the FTU (formal training unit) for the F-117 type, and in 1994 renamed as the Screamin Demons, although the badge was retained. The 7th FS became the 7th Combat Training Squadron (CTS). In addition to the previous duties of initial F-117 pilot certification, the 7th picked up the academic training for the F-117. The 7th CTS was redesignated as the 7th FS on 22 July 2005. As a result of the planned retirement of the F-117 there was no longer a need to train F-117 pilots. This resulted in the inactivation of the 7th FS on 15 December 2006. It was activated as the first Holloman F-22 Squadron on 15 May 2008.

8th Fighter Squadron Black Sheep

The 8th Fighter Squadron Black Sheep took over the F-117 operations of the former 416th FS (Ghostriders) on 30 July 1993. The squadron emblem is a silhouette of a black sheep inside a golden yellow circle bordered in black. The squadron began as the 8th Pursuit Squadron (Interceptor) on 20 November 1940 with Seversky P-35s. The squadron's history includes combat in New Guinea and the Philippines in P-40s, P-47s and P-38s; in Korea in F-80s and F-84s; and Cold War operations with the F-100, F-105, F-4 and F-15. The 8th FS was primarily tasked against Pacific theater commitments and would have been the first F-117 squadron deployed to Korea in event of a crisis there.

9th Fighter Squadron Iron Knights

The 9th Fighter Squadron Iron Knights took over the F-117 operations of the former 415th Fighter Squadron Nighthawks (formerly Nightstalkers) on 30 July 1993. The squadron emblem is a white, winged knight's helmet on a blue disk bordered in black, and began as the 9th Pursuit Squadron (Interceptor) on 20 November 1940 with Seversky P-35s. The history includes combat in New Guinea and the Philippines in P-40s, P-47s and P-38s; in Korea in F-80s and F-84s; and Cold War operations with the F-100, F-105, F-4 and F-15. The 9th FS was primarily tasked against European theater commitments and would have been the first F-117 squadron deployed to Europe in event of a crisis there.

F-117 85-0816, marked as the 7 FS jet over Holloman with the F-117 hangars in the upper left. (Lockheed Martin Aeronautics Company)

57TH WING NELLIS AFB, NEVADA

57th Fighter Weapons Wing

The 57th Fighter Weapons Wing at Nellis AFB, Nevada, conducted weapons, armament and tactics tests and training for the USAF's Tactical Air Command (TAC). In addition to maintaining squadrons at Nellis for various aircraft types (F-16, F-111, A-10), the 57th Wing has traditionally operated detachments at air bases in connection with less numerous types. Weaponeering with the Senior Trend F-117 aircraft had been performed in the black world by the 4450th Tactical Group until 5 October 1989, when (on the same day the 4450th TG became the 37th TFW) TAC activated Detachment 1, 57th FWW, at the Tonopah Test Range, Nevada. Typically, the detachment flew F-117 aircraft based at Tonopah, but carried out everyday operations, no longer constrained by blackness, in better-known sectors of the Nellis reservation.

The 57th FWW detachment remained in operation on 1 October 1991 when its parent unit was redesignated 57th Fighter Wing. The 57th Fighter Wing acquired its new designation and continued to operate its Detachment 1 at Tonopah. After the F-117 force relocated from Tonopah to Holloman, Detachment 1, now known as the Dragon Test Team, was activated at Holloman on 1 June 1992, the date TAC became Air Combat Command (ACC), and roughly coinciding with the beginning of F-117 operations on 5 July 1992. Typically, the Dragon Test Team operated two or three F-117s at Holloman with WA tail codes but flew to Nellis for most weapon tests and training.

A new change in designation for the 57th FWW took place, making it the 57th Wing, on 1 February 1993. The change was made because the wing had expanded to encompass much more than simply fighters. By this time, the USAF Weapons School, a major part of the wing, had added bombers to its growing stable that also included AWACS and other non-fighter divisions. The wing also controlled other diverse operations such as Air Warrior, added a combat search and rescue squadron at the same time, and soon after would begin adding Predator UAV squadrons. The 57th Wing's Detachment 1, alias the Dragon Test Team, continued to operate two or three F-117s at Holloman with WA tail codes and took the aircraft to Nellis for most weapon tests and training. The 57th Wing had an OL (operating location) at Kirtland AFB, New Mexico, where various aircraft types including the F-117 have been evaluated for their vulnerability to EMP (electromagnetic pulse).

Det. 5, USAF Weapons School (F-117 Division) /417th Weapons Squadron

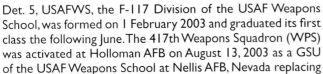

Det. 5, USAFWS, the F-117 Division of the USAF Weapons School, was formed on 1 February 2003 and graduated its first class the following June. The 417th Weapons Squadron (WPS) was activated at Holloman AFB on August 13, 2003 as a GSU of the USAF Weapons School at Nellis AFB, Nevada replacing the F-117 detachment. The 417th WPS operated at Holloman AFB using aircraft and resources of the 49th Fighter Wing. As a result of the planned retirement of the F-117, the 417 WPS was inactivated on 15 September 2006 after graduating its last class in June of 2006.

Detachment 1 53rd Test and Evaluation Group (TEG)

Detachment 1, 79th Test Evaluation Group, stationed at Holloman AFB was the only Air Combat Command unit that owns an F-117 outside of the reaches of the Fightin' 49ers (49th FW). The Dragon Test Team operated a single F-117A from Holloman AFB. The unit that owned Detachment 1, the 79th TEG, was based at Eglin Air Force Base, Florida, and belonged to Eglin's 53rd Wing. The Dragon aircraft was maintained by the 7th FS and its tail code was that of the 53rd Wing – OT. It was a task of the detachment to take what was developed at the Lockheed-Martin facility in Palmdale, Calif., Follow-on Operational Test & Evaluation (FOT&E) and test it at the operational flying level (IOT&E). On 20 November 1998 the 79th TEG became the 53rd TEG, and the Dragon Test Team became Det. 1, 53rd TEG, 53rd Wing. The 53rd Test and Evaluation Group was responsible for the overall management of the 53rd Wing's flying activities. Det. 1 was inactivated on 1 October 2006 and the Dragon aircraft (85-0835) was retired to Tonopah on 13 March 2007 as part of the first group of F-117s to be retired.

422nd Test and Evaluation Squadron

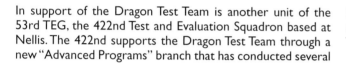

In support of the Dragon Test Team is another unit of the 53rd TEG, the 422nd Test and Evaluation Squadron based at Nellis. The 422nd supports the Dragon Test Team through a new "Advanced Programs" branch that has conducted several important foreign materiel exploitation projects and provided support to the F-22, B-2, and F-117A (through the Dragon Test Team) programs.

85-0835, the Gray Dragon, assigned to Det I, 53 TEG, rotates for takeoff 13 March 2007 for its retirement flight. (USAF)

412TH TEST WING EDWARDS AFB, CALIFORNIA

The 412th Test Wing at Edwards AFB is the parent organization of the 410th Test Squadron.

410th Flight Test Squadron (ED), Palmdale, California

The 410th Test Squadron acquired its designation on 1 May 1993 at the Palmdale Skunk Works flight test center. The 410th TS traces its roots, if not its formal lineage, to the 4450th Tactical Group's Q-Unit, test outfit during the early Tonopah era, activated with the group on 15 October 1979 as a small flight test detachment that apparently kept a handful of test pilots at Groom Lake. From the earliest days of the black Senior Trend program, the USAF maintained a detachment of test pilots at Lockheed's Burbank Skunk Works, where operational pilots went through an initial ground-training course. As an acceptance and test squadron with no name, the unit also operated at Groom Lake in early days, where the Baja scorpion was adopted as the symbol of the Lockheed-USAF development effort; the unit then moved to Tonopah with the rest of the F-117 community. Q-Unit was inactivated on 30 May 1989.

The Palmdale F-117 flight test unit, which was subordinate to the 412th Test Wing (previously 6510th Test Wing) at Edwards AFB, California operated without any designation from 1989 onward, and moved from Tonopah to Palmdale (rather than to Holloman, with the rest of the F-117 force) in March 1992. It was designated 410th Flight Test Squadron (FLTS) on 1 March 1993 and operated five F-117s (79-10782, 79-10783, 79-10784, 84-0811, and 85-0831, the first three being the surviving full-scale development aircraft). 782 and 783 were retired in early 2008 becoming static display aircraft at Holloman and Palmdale respectively. 84-0828 and 88-0841 were assigned to the CTF as replacements until summer 2008.

On 1 August 2008, after more than 27 years and 8,000 flight test hours, the 410th Flight Test Squadron was inactivated at the U.S. Air Force Plant 42 in Palmdale. The final formation flight of F-117 Night Hawks took place on 6 August from Palmdale with two of the inactivated 410th F-117s. On Monday, 11 August, 831 taxied to Palmdale's Runway 25 and took off for the final flight of an F-117. Turning just after takeoff 831 did three low passes over the 410th FLTS facility, and then flew on to Tonopah, Nevada, closing the book on the F-117.

F-117 PILOT TRAINING

Pilot Training at Tonopah

Initially, because of the secrecy involved with the F-117 program, perspective pilots were often found based on personal recommendations from current Bandits, Wing commanders, and recommendations from the individual Commands (SAC and TAC) themselves. Minimum qualification for being an F-117 pilot included a stellar record of performance, a rank of Capt. (often Maj.), at least one tour as an instructor pilot, and over 1,000 hours (many over 2,000 hours) of command pilot flight experience. Pilots selected for the F-117 program often had experience in the F-111, F-15, F-16, or A-10. Many pilots had held positions such as chief of tactics, flight examiner, or flight commander at their former assignments. Even with all of these credentials, a perspective F-117 pilot would have to go through almost a year of training before making their first flight in the Black Jet.

Aviators joining the 4450th TG during the days when the program was "black" were first sent to Tucson International Airport where the 162nd Tactical Fighter Group, Arizona Air National Guard, trained A-7 pilots for the Air National Guard. The 4450th TG was only active duty USAF unit still using the A-7. The 4450th TG pilots stuck out in the crowd during the four month long training, and the Air National Guard pilots soon heard rumors of this mysterious unit flying A-7s that had a classified mission. Then to Nellis for a local-area check out by the Nellis based A-7 Instructor Pilots (IPs). The local area checkout consisted of five or six rides, flying around Nellis Ranges and some low level; basically showing how to fly around the local area. It is at this point that the pilots where told their real assignment-flying the F-117. The training was accomplished by the 4451st TS as part of the 4450th TG and

later by the 417th TFTS/FS Bandits part of the 37th TFW/FW at Tonopah.

The soon to be Bandits next went through the academic and simulator training specific to the F-117. Because of the backlog of training pilots, it would often be as much as five months from finishing A-7 training to starting F-117 academic training. After academic training was cockpit mock-up and simulator training. One of the final things that pilots would do before making their first F-117 flight was a high speed, no flap landing in a USAF F-15. The pilots would go to Luke AFB and undergo two days of academics and simulator instruction-all for one ride in an F-15. It was thought that this best simulated the landing profile that these pilots would experience in the F-117. Because the F-117 only has one seat and there are no trainer versions, the new pilot has to be able to land it safely the first time. After almost a year in training a prospective 4450th TG pilot would have his first opportunity to fly the F-117 – in daytime.

After the existence of the F-117 was revealed, training procedures were modified slightly. The older A-7's were replaced by more common place T-38's. At first the perspective would go to Holloman AFB (Ironically, the future home for the F-117) to get landing currency in the AT-38. The students got three sorties in the AT-38, and then went to Tonopah for computer-based and contractor-taught academics and a host of simulator missions. Before even being allowed to taxi an F-117, new pilots had to go through a three-stepped training process that taught the pilot the cockpit of the F-117. The first step was the computer-based training (CBT). The CBT program used SUN workstations hooked up to a touch

37th FW F-117 and T-38 over the Nevada desert. (USAF)

screen monitor with switch positions in the graphics. The second step was the cockpit procedures trainer, the Part Task Trainer (PTT). The PTT was used aquatint new pilots with the F-117 switches and controls. Getting the switch locations down even before flying the simulator was a necessity. Next came the training in the F-117 flight simulator.

CAE-Link Corp. in Binghamton, N.Y. built two F-117 flight simulators. The first simulator was the weapons system trainer (WST). The WST entered service at Nellis AFB in January 1987 and then moved to Holloman with the relocation of the F-117 Wing. The contract to build the simulator was awarded in August 1982.

The second simulator was at the CAE-Link Corp. plant in Binghamton, N.Y. The CAE-Links simulator in Binghamton checks out new or upgraded equipment before it's installed in the airplanes. The simulator has helped catch some design glitches that could have affected the aircraft's performance. Using the system for debugging new hardware and software also avoids tying up the other F-117 simulator the company has built; the WST used for pilot training.

After completing the required hours in the simulator, and various written exams, the pilots were finally allowed to taxi the F-117. The very first thing done was an intentionally-aborted takeoff in the F-117 to practice popping the drag chute, then finally their first flight in the Black Jet, all of which had to happen within the forty-five days since they landed the AT-38 at Holloman. All the initial qualification F-117 sorties were chased by Tonopah T-38s with an instructor on board to talk pilots through everything. The first flight was in full daylight and VMC (Visual Meteorological Condition) with instructor pilots chasing in a T-38. Pilots got at least twelve sorties in day/VMC before flying at night, as well as a lot of night simulator time. When a pilot became F-117 qualified, he received an individual Bandit number and a medallion. There have been a total of 509 operational pilots trained at both Tonopah and Holloman receiving bandit numbers from 150 to 708.

Once F-117 qualified, Bandits must next become mission qualified. The Bandit would leave the training squadron and be assigned to one of the two operational squadrons. Here they would become mission qualified by learning tactics while flying training missions. Once mission qualified, the full-fledged Bandit was ready to deploy with the F-117 and if necessary, employ the training he has received in combat.

Pilot Training at Holloman
With the relocation of the F-117 Wing to Holloman, F-117 pilot training naturally moved with the wing. Initially the 49th Training Squadron was responsible for the F-117 academic training, and the 7th FS "Screamin Demons" was responsible the simulator training and Bandit qualification. In early 1999, the 49th TS was inactivated, and the 7th FS became the 7th Combat Training Squadron (CTS). In addition to the previous duties of initial F-117 pilot certification, the 7th picked up the academic training for the F-117. The nine F-117's assigned to the 7th FS were transferred to the 9th FS and the 9th's assigned aircraft was increased from eighteen aircraft to twenty-four aircraft. The fifteen A/T-38's remained assigned to the 7th CTS. The 7th CTS was redesignated as the 7th FS on 22 July 2005. As the F-117 program wound down approaching the retirement of the F-117 fleet, the need for new pilots decreased and the 7th FS was inactivated on 15 December 2006.

F-117 OPERATIONS SITES

Lockheed Advanced Development Company (Skunk Works) PS-11

Located in Burbank, California, the Lockheed Skunk Works (PS-11) was the birthplace of the F-117 aircraft. Skunk Works is the nickname for Lockheed Martin Aeronautics' Advanced Development Company, the birthplace of the F-117. The name Skunk Works came from Al Capp's Li'l Abner comic strip, which featured the "skonk works," where Appalachian hillbillies ground up skunks, old shoes, and other foul-smelling ingredients to brew fearsome drinks and other products. To hide its true nature, Lockheed engineers identified the secret XP-80 assembly shed – which ironically was across the street from a malodorous plastics factory – as the place where Kelly Johnson was stirring up some kind of potent brew. The nickname stuck, although skonk became skunk in deference to the non-hillbillies working at the top-secret facility and because Capp objected to anyone else using his unique spelling. Cartoonist Capp and his Li'l Abner comic strip departed many years ago, but the Skunk Works – a registered service mark of Lockheed Martin Corporation along with the familiar skunk logo – lives on as Lockheed Martin Aeronautics Company continues to "brew" the world's most potent aircraft.

The Skunk Works began working on stealth as far back as the late-1950s, and low radar observability had played a role in the design of the A-12/YF-12/SR-71 series of Mach 3+ aircraft. The F-117A was the first warplane to be specifically designed from the outset for low radar observability. The gain of valuable engineering data during the Have Blue flight test program led to a Full Scale Development (FSD) decision by the Air Force. A contract was awarded to the Lockheed Skunk Works on November 16, 1978. The original order was for five FSD test aircraft and fifteen production articles. The initial F-117, Aircraft 780, was delivered 28 April 1981 and subsequent production lots of varying quantities yielded a total of sixty-four aircraft built and delivered through June 27, 1990.

Detachment 3 (or Det. 3), AFFTC – Groom Lake, Nevada

The test site located at Groom Dry Lake has been known by many names since its construction. Lockheed's Kelly Johnson named the place "Paradise Ranch" hoping to fool employees into working at a place with such a pleasant name. When his flight test team arrived in July 1955, they simply called it "The Ranch". The secret base was formally named Watertown Strip, after the town in upstate New York where CIA director Allen Dulles was born. In June 1958, it was officially designated Area 51 by the Atomic Energy Commission (AEC). The adjacent AEC proving grounds became known as the Nevada Test Site and divided into numbered areas. By 1970, the USAF Systems Command took over the operation of Groom Lake. Its designation was officially changed to Detachment 3 (or Det. 3), AFFTC (based at Edwards AFB). Despite this fact, the older name Area 51 has been popularized by the mass media and Hollywood and is a part of pop culture.

In 1975, the Red Flag series of realistic air warfare exercises started at Nellis AFB, using large portions of the ranges surrounding Groom Lake. The box of airspace surrounding Groom Lake was strictly off-limits to Red Flag and Nellis based aircrews. It became known informally as "Red Square" at this time (because acquired Soviet aircraft were being test flown there at the time by the Red Eagles).

Later the base acquired the semi-official title of Dreamland as a series of new exotic aerospace projects evolved in the late 1970s. These included the Have Blue/XST and Tacit Blue stealth technology demonstrators. The testing of these aircraft brought the extreme security measures at Groom Lake that we see today. All fifty-two Have Blue test flights occurred at Groom Lake. Both Have Blue crashes occurred on the surrounding ranges, and the wreckages of both aircraft are buried in the Groom Lake vicinity.

Tonopah Test Range Airfield, Nevada (PS 66)

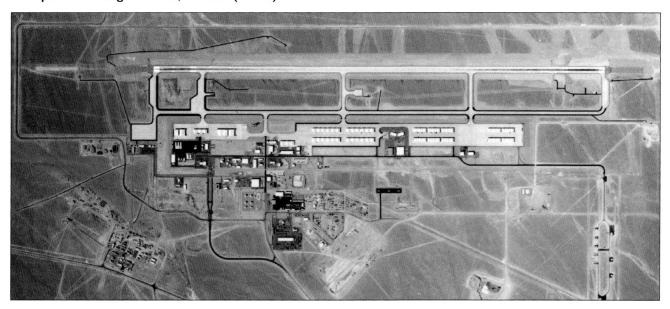

The 4450 TG began flying operations in 1981 from the Tonopah Test Range Airfield, located approximately 130 miles northwest of Las Vegas, Nevada. Lockheed test pilots put the Stealth Fighter through its early paces. The 4450 TG also operated the A-7D as a surrogate trainer for the F-117, and these operations continued until 15 October 1982 under the guise of an avionics test mission. On October 15th Major Alton C. Whitley, Jr. became the first 4450 TG pilot to fly the F-117. The 4450 TG then achieved an initial operating capability with the F-117 in October 1983.

The 4450 TG's mission continued to evolve under a cloak of secrecy – all Tonopah training flights conducted at night under the cover of darkness – until late 1988. On 10 November 1988, the Air Force brought the F-117 from behind a "black veil" by publicly acknowledging its existence. In January 1989, the AT-38 replaced the A-7 in the unit's inventory as a measure to streamline the F-117's training operation. On 5 October 1989, TAC inactivated the 4450 TG and all subordinate units, and concurrently moved the 37th Tactical Fighter Wing (TFW) from George AFB, California, to Tonopah to assume the F-117 mission. The 37 TFW capped 1989's achievements on 20 December by taking the F-117 on its first combat mission: Operation JUST CAUSE. Since then, the 37 TFW has also taken the F-117 to Nellis AFB on 21 April 1990 for its first public display and to England AFB, Louisiana, in late June 1990 for its first deployment to another base in the United States.

A 37th FW F-117 taxis out from the hangar complex at Tonopah Test Range Airfield. (USAF)

Holloman AFB, New Mexico

A four ship of 49th FW F-117 waits to take the runway for takeoff. (USAF)

The 49th Fighter Wing took over the F-117 squadrons and the equipment and personnel of the dismantled 37th Fighter Wing when the move from Tonopah to Holloman AFB, New Mexico, was made on 5 July 1992. While at Holloman the F-117s flew combat missions in support of Desert Storm, Southern Watch, Provide Comfort, Operation Allied Force in Kosovo, and Operation Iraqi Freedom. F-117 operations started to wind down in 2006 with the inactivation of the 417 Weapons Squadron and the Dragon Test tea. On 13 March 2007 the first six F-117s left Holloman for storage at Tonopah, with the last four departing Holloman on 22 April 2008. A new chapter started for the 49th Fighter Wing with the arrival of its first F-22 Raptors on 2 June 2008.

F-117 85-0816, marked as the 7 FS Flagship over Holloman the hangars built for the F-117s at Holloman. (Lockheed Martin Aeronautics Company)

Lockheed Palmdale Plant 10 PS-77

A depot was established in 1984 to accomplish repairs and install modifications on the aircraft. This depot, first located in Lockheed's Palmdale Plant 10 (PS-77), eventually took the place of Lockheed Depot Field Teams performing the depot work on site at Tonopah (PS-66). Half of an existing Lockheed hangar, Building 602, was secured, and appropriate fencing was installed around it, including a taxiway gate to allow C-5s into the vicinity of the building for loading and unloading. This enabled the concept of Compatibility Updates (CU's) to be implemented, in which an attempt was made to create blocks of aircraft having the same or similar configurations.

The F-117s were moved to and from the depot by C-5 at night in order to maintain program security. This meant that the aircraft had to be defueled, disassembled, cradled, and then loaded aboard the C-5, flown to the depot, and unloaded before the real work could begin. Of course, this meant that the reverse actions had to occur at the end of the depot work before the article could be reassembled, flight-tested, and redelivered to the operating Group.

Another limitation, caused by the need for secrecy, was that the articles could not be moved around outside of Building 602 for the same reason they could not be flown to and from Palmdale. This meant that a separate facility for fueling/defueling operations was impractical, so articles in work, and the depot building itself, smelled strongly of jet fuel. This caused some concern for the safety of the operation. The solution to that problem was to move the depot to Site 7 of Air Force Plant 42, adjacent to the Lockheed plant in Palmdale, as soon as possible. The Combined Test Force (CTF) was also eventually moved to the same site. This co-location allowed synergies and economies among the Lockheed support personnel.

Home of the F-117's flight test unit is Site 7, Air Force Plant 42 in Palmdale, California (Lockheed Martin Aeronautics Company)

The twenty-five ship is seen approaching the reviewing stand in Heritage Park at Holloman AFB. (Lockheed Martin Aeronautics Company)

F-117 Aircraft

F-117 Tail Number/Serial Number Listing

F-117 serial numbers are unique in that they were assigned after production was complete. Since the program was a "black" classified program at the time of manufacture of the aircraft, the F-117 aircraft received tail numbers running from 777 through 843 instead of standard DoD serial numbers. 777, 778, and 779 were pulled off the assembly line after the construction of 780 began and were non-flyable static test airframes. 780 through 843 were the numbers assigned to the FSD and production aircraft. When the program was declassified the operational aircraft received unused serial numbers from the existing 1979, 1980, 1981, 1982, 1983, 1984, 1985, 1986, and 1988 year groups.

The 'I' was added in front of the last four digits of the tail number for aircraft 793 thru 798 in 1992 after it was discovered that those aircraft had duplicate serial numbers with some F-16s in the Air Force fleet. HQ ACC changed the numbers so that maintenance data could be entered into the CAMS (Consolidated Aircraft Maintenance System) database to track maintenance data.

Tail No	Serial No	Organization
PRODUCTION LOT 1		
FSD (Full System Development) Aircraft		
780	79-0780	Orig CTF
781	79-0781	Orig CTF
782	79-0782	412 TW
783	79-0783	412 TW
784	79-0784	412 TW
PRODUCTION LOT 2		
785	79-0785	Lockheed*
786	80-0786	49FW
787	80-0787	49FW
788	80-0788	49FW
789	80-0789	49FW
790	80-0790	49FW
791	80-0791	49FW
PRODUCTION LOT 3		
792	80-0792	4450TG*
793	81-10793	49FW*
794	81-10794	49FW
795	81-10795	49FW
796	81-10796	49FW
797	81-10797	49FW
798	81-10798	49FW

Tail No	Serial No	Organization
PRODUCTION LOT 4		
799	82-0799	49FW
800	82-0800	49FW
801	82-0801	49FW*
802	82-0802	49FW
803	82-0803	49FW
804	82-0804	49FW
805	82-0805	49FW
806	82-0806	49FW
PRODUCTION LOT 5		
807	83-0807	49FW
808	83-0808	49FW
809	84-0809	49FW
810	84-0810	49FW
PRODUCTION LOT 6		
811	84-0811	412 TW
812	84-0812	49FW
PRODUCTION LOT 7		
813	85-0813	49FW
814	85-0814	49FW
815	85-0815	4450TG*
816	85-0816	49FW
817	85-0817	49FW
818	85-0818	49FW
819	85-0819	49FW

* Aircraft was assigned to the organization when it crashed.

Tail No	Serial No	Organization	Tail No	Serial No	Organization
PRODUCTION LOT 8			**PRODUCTION LOT 10**		
820	85-0820	49FW	837	86-0837	49FW
821	86-0821	49FW	838	86-0838	49FW
822	86-0822	49FW	839	86-0839	49FW
823	86-0823	49FW	840	86-0840	49FW
824	84-0824	49FW			
825	84-0825	49FW	**PRODUCTION LOT 11**		
826	84-0826	49FW	841	88-0841	49FW
827	84-0827	49FW	842	88-0842	49FW
828	84-0828	49FW	843	88-0843	49FW
PRODUCTION LOT 9					
829	85-0829	49FW			
830	85-0830	49FW			
831	85-0831	412 TW			
832	85-0832	49FW			
833	85-0833	49FW			
834	85-0834	49FW			
835	85-0835	53d WG			
836	85-0836	49FW			

85-0835 over a flooded part of the White Sands National Monument on 27 August 2006. (Jim Haseltine Photo)

HAVE BLUE AIRCRAFT

XST-1 Have Blue 01

The first flight of Have Blue occurred on 1 December 1977 with Bill Park at the controls. The aircraft crashed on 4 May 1978 when a damaged right main landing gear did not extend. Rather than try to land with only the left main landing gear, the pilot attempted to lower the gear, but was unsuccessful. The pilot ejected at approximately 10,000 feet when the jet ran out of fuel. The aircraft was destroyed on impact with the ground in the vicinity of the Groom Lake facility.

Lockheed's Have Blue 01 sits on the ramp at the test site. Mike Kammerer can be seen in the cockpit. The camouflage paint scheme was one of many that were tested on the two Have Blue prototypes during the test program. (Lockheed Martin Aeronautics Company)

(Lockheed Martin Aeronautics Company)

XST-2 Have Blue 02

Have Blue 02 first flight on 20 July 1978. It was flown by Lt.Col. Ken Dyson pilot. The aircraft crashed in July 1979. A hydraulic leak caused an engine fire. Due to hydraulic failure aircraft pitched up and down violently and could not be controlled. Pilot ejected. The aircraft was destroyed on impact with the ground on the Tonopah test range thirty-five miles North West of the Groom Lake facility.

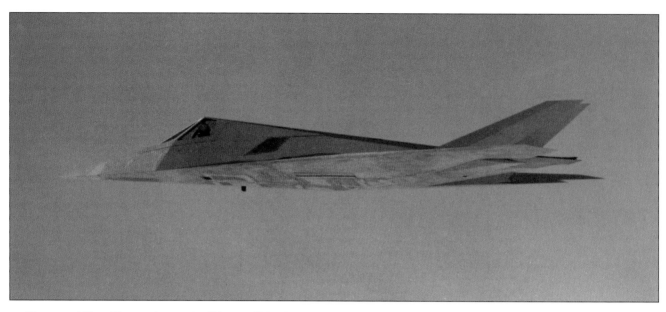

The second Have Blue made a total of fifty-two flights between July 1978 and July 1979. (Lockheed Martin Aeronautics Company)

The two Have Blue prototypes were identical. Here the second prototype sits in a hangar at the Lockheed facility in Burbank prior to being shipped to the test site. The aircraft has its wingtips removed so it will fit into the C-5 aircraft for shipment. (Lockheed Martin Aeronautics Company)

STATIC TEST AIRFRAMES

777

Airframe 777 was initially used as a structural test article. After those tests were complete the airframe was restored to be used as a Radar Cross Section pole model. The airframe was modified with a fifty-three inch hole in the Center for a rotation device to be installed and could be mounted on the pole from either the top or the bottom.

777 F-117 airframe is seen here before the structural tests. (Lockheed Martin Aeronautics Company)

777 is seen here being placed on a pole, and after installed on the pole for RCS testing. (Lockheed Martin Aeronautics Company)

778
Static Tests – No Photo available.

779
Airframe 779 was a mid-section used for weapon bay tests. Later it was used as a structural test article. The red stress test rig can be seen directly behind the airframe.

Airframe 779 is seen here being readied for mounting in the stress test rig (above) and mounted in the rig (below). (Lockheed Martin Aeronautics Company)

(Lockheed Martin Aeronautics Company)

FULL SYSTEM DEVELOPMENT (FSD) LOT I NIGHT HAWKS

780 – 79-0780

Scorpion 1, Full-Scale Development (FSD) aircraft was delivered to the USAF on 10 June 1981. 780 first flew on 18 June 1981, at Groom Dry Lake, Nevada piloted by Hal Farley. FSD-1 was used for most testing related to the basic air vehicle. It was delivered unpainted, but made its first flight in desert camouflage. Its initial configuration included the conventional nose boom, and small vertical fins. The small verticals were replaced after the tenth flight (August 6, 1981). It initially flew with the larger fins on October 21, 1981. The aircraft lost a tail fin during a sideslip in 1987 but landed safely. It was positioned by the Nellis Boulevard gate at Nellis Air Force Base, Nevada on May 16, 1992. This was the first of the F-117A series to take up gate guardian duties.

780 wore this camouflage for the first ten flights and then was painted gray. (Lockheed Martin Aeronautics Company)

(Lockheed Martin Aeronautics Company)

(Lockheed Martin Aeronautics Company)

780 is seen here with the right weapons bay door open. The orange fairing under the wing contains cameras to film the weapons bay. The left bay was filled with instrumentation and the door was not opened in flight. (Lockheed Martin Aeronautics Company)

780 is seen here in its hangar at the test site painted light gray. (Lockheed Martin Aeronautics Company)

(Lockheed Martin Aeronautics Company)

(Lockheed Martin Aeronautics Company)

780 carried special markings such as crew names and a "Scorpion I" logo. (Lockheed Martin Aeronautics Company)

Starting on 14 December 1983, leading edge extensions were tested on 780 in an attempt to reduce landing and takeoff speeds. Barely visible painted on the bottom is a silhouette of the F-117. (Lockheed Martin Aeronautics Company)

After it final flight on 11 April 1985, 780 was placed in storage. It had made 137th test flights during its four year career. It was placed on display at Nellis AFB on May 16, 1992, positioned by the Nellis Boulevard gate. This was the first of the F-117A series to take up gate guardian duties. (Don Logan Photo)

781 – 79-0781

Scorpion, the second FSD aircraft made its first flight 4 September 1981. It made its first flight unpainted. On 18 December 1981 it was delivered to the USAF. It was originally configured with the conventional nose boom and small tail fins and was retrofitted with larger fins after four flights. During the retrofit, a production nose assembly was also installed. The first SENIOR TREND RCS test flight occurred on 23 January 1982. This aircraft was used for weapons separation, anti-icing, flying qualities, and performance testing. It reportedly carried a White Playboy Bunny on the fin during testing. It was delivered to the National Museum of U.S. Air Force Museum at Wright Patterson AFB on 17 July 1991 and is now preserved on display at the Museum.

Prior to being shipped to the National Museum of the U.S. Air Force, 781 was bead blasted of all its radar absorbent coatings. The stripped aircraft made a functional test flight on 27 June 1991 marked with "TOXIC DEATH" on both sides as seen here. (Lockheed Martin Aeronautics Company)

781 is seen here on the ramp at National Museum of the U.S. Air Force, prior to being moved inside. (Dave Menard Photo)

782 – 79-0782

Scorpion 3 FSD aircraft first flew on 18 December 1981. It was used for acoustics and navigation system testing. Initially painted gray, 782 was delivered to the USAF on 21 April 1982. In November 1983 the aircraft was painted with a U.S. flag motif on the underside. The reason for this – the aircraft was officially being unveiled to high-ranking officials, including Secretary of Defense Caspar Weinberger during a F-117A test force change of command ceremony at Groom Lake on 14 December 1983. The flag remained on the aircraft until March 1984. On 5 April 2008 782 was placed on permanent static display at Holloman

In November 1983 the aircraft was painted with a U.S. flag motif on the underside. The reason for this- the aircraft was officially being unveiled to high-ranking officials, including Secretary of Defense Caspar Weinberger during a F-117A test force change of command ceremony at Groom Lake on 14 December 1983. The flag remained on the aircraft until March 1984. (Lockheed Martin Aeronautics Company)

782 in 410 Test Squadron markings at Edwards AFB 3 October 1998. (Craig Kaston Photo)

After the flag was removed flight test personnel wanted another unique paint job. In 1986 the "Baja Scorpions" logo was painted on the bottom of 782. This logo stayed on the aircraft until 1989. (Lockheed Martin Aeronautics Company)

(Lockheed Martin Aeronautics Company)

Under program "Evening Shade" from 12 July to 7th October 1993 782 was painted gray for daylight visibility tests (opposite bottom, above and below). It used the call sign "Gray Ghost" and was painted back to black prior to an appearance at the Edwards AFB 1993 Open House. (Lockheed Martin Aeronautics Company)

(Lockheed Martin Aeronautics Company)

(Lockheed Martin Aeronautics Company)

782 flies over snow capped mountains of Southern California during February 2001. (Lockheed Martin Aeronautics Company photo by Judson Brohmer)

One of the last weapons to be tested on the F-117 was the Joint Air to Surface Standoff Missile (JASSM). The F-117 could carry a single JASSM in each weapons bay. 782 was used for the initial fit checks of the missile. (Lockheed Martin Aeronautics Company)

(Lockheed Martin Aeronautics Company photo by Judson Brohmer)

(Lockheed Martin Aeronautics Company photo by Judson Brohmer)

In October 2005 the Air Force decided to retire 782. It had flown more than 1,200 flights and 1,500 flying hours during its twenty-four-year career with the 410 TS. It was repainted with the U.S. flag on its underside. In November 2006. the aircraft was painted with a U.S. flag motif on the underside as seen here at the Edwards AFB Open House on 24 November 2006. (Pete Snowden Photo)

782 was flown to Holloman where it was used as a maintenance trainer. In early 2008 was prepared for permanent static display at Holloman and was painted as 85-0816, the world's first stealth aircraft to employ ordinance in combat in both Operations Just Cause and Desert Storm. On both occasions the aircraft was piloted by Major Gregory "Beast" Feest. (USAF)

On 5 April 2008, 782, painted as 816 was moved to Holloman's Heritage Park for display (above and below). (USAF)

(USAF)

783 – 79-0783

Scorpion 4 FSD aircraft was initially delivered in early 1982. 783 remained grounded for RCS configuration testing until its first flight on 7 July 1982. It was used for RCS and IR signature testing. It was delivered to the USAF on 5 August 1982 and was later used for avionics integration tests. During the early Senior Trend years FSD-4 had its own patch, a red delta shape with the number "4" and a black scorpion superimposed over it. The patch shape was based on the wing shape of the F-117. On 3 March 2008 it was moved to Blackbird Airpark at Palmdale airport and placed on permanent static display.

783 is seen here being hoisted onto a pylon for **RCS** configuration testing in early 1982. (**Lockheed Martin Aeronautics Company**)

783 in 410 Test Squadron markings at Edwards AFB 18 October 1992. (Craig Kaston Photo)

783 in 410 Test Squadron markings at Edwards AFB 10 October 1999. (Tim Hunter Photo)

783 at Palmdale 6 December 2003. (Lockheed Martin Aeronautics Company photo by Denny Lombard)

During 2007, 783 was painted in the two gray scheme also used by the Dragon Test team on 835 seen at the Barksdale AFB air show on 14 May 2005 (above and opposite). (Matt Ellis Photo)

In early 2008 it was repainted to black and prepared for static display. On 3 March 2008 it was moved to Blackbird Airpark at Palmdale airport and placed next to the Lockheed A-12 on display there along with an SR-71 and D-21 drone (above and below). (USAF)

(USAF)

784 – 79-0784

Scorpion 5 FSD aircraft first flew on 10 April 1982 and was delivered to the USAF on 22 June 1982. 784 was displayed for Secretary of Defense Caspar Weinberger during a secret visit to Groom Lake in 1984. Used for navigation/autopilot and avionics development. During July 1993 784, as part of a program called SENIOR SPUD, had the left side of the fuselage and the inside of the vertical stabilizers covered in a textured metallic surface. The aircraft made a total of four flights prior to the coatings being removed.

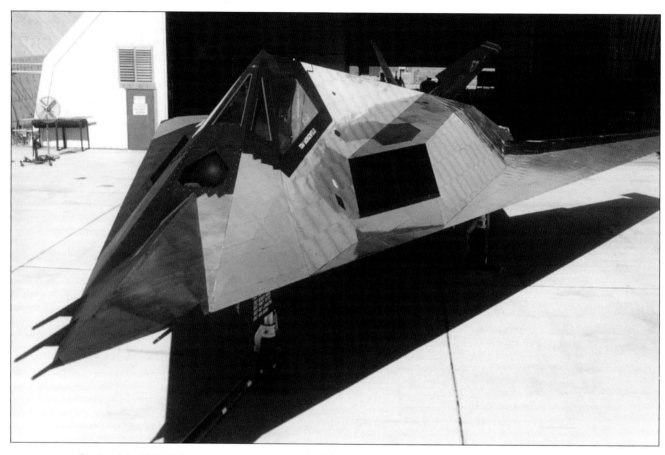

During July 1993 784, as part of a program called **SENIOR SPUD**, had the left side of the fuselage and the inside of the vertical stabilizers covered in a textured metallic surface. (Lockheed Martin Aeronautics Company)

The gray stripe on the right wing was an early gray paint being developed for the F-22. (Lockheed Martin Aeronautics Company)

The aircraft made a total of four flights prior to the coatings being removed. (Lockheed Martin Aeronautics Company)

783 seen from below at the Edwards Air Show on 28 October 2006. (Matt Ellis Photo)

(Lockheed Martin Aeronautics Company)

Night Hawks May 2000. (Lockheed Martin Aeronautics Company photo by Judson Brohmer)

Four F-117s of the 410th Flight Test Squadron over the Antelope Valley south of Edwards AFB. Stacked top to bottom are; 79-10784, 79-10783, 84-0811, and 85-0831. (USAF photo by Bobbi Taplin)

784 and 782 over Palmdale (Lockheed Martin Aeronautics Company)

On Tuesday, 26 April 2008 the last F-117 remaining at Palmdale (FSD aircraft 784), was unceremoniously scrapped. The edge RAM treatments were removed and the airframe was broken up and crushed. 784 was considered a proof of concept study for finding an effective method of destroying F-117A airframes. (Lockheed Martin Aeronautics Company)

(Lockheed Martin Aeronautics Company)

PRODUCTION LOT 2 NIGHT HAWKS

785 – 79-0785

Crashed 20 April 1982 prior to U.S. Air Force acceptance (Robert L. Riedenauer pilot), the flight control system had been assembled incorrectly during manufacture of the aircraft at Burbank. A major design change in the system caught Lockheed workers off guard: the input points on the flight control computer were placed in a different sequence than they had been on the previous version. As a result the aircraft went out of control and crashed on takeoff. The pilot did not have time to eject. He was badly injured and hospitalized for eight months. He was forced to retire from flying. The battered airframe of 785 was returned to Lockheed Skunk Works in Burbank as a functional engineering airframe test fixture used to test the fit of new components.

The battered airframe of 785 was returned to Lockheed Skunk Works in Burbank as a functional engineering airframe test fixture used to test the fit of new components. (Lockheed Martin Aeronautics Company)

786 – 80-0786

WAR PIG first flew on 15 July 1982 and was accepted by the Air Force on 2 September 1982. It was the first operational aircraft delivered. It was used initially for weapons tests until assigned to the 4450th TG in September 1982. 786 was the first F-117 to see combat. During Desert Storm 786 flew twenty-four combat missions while 416th TFS. On 4 April 1999

786, then assigned to the 9th FS deployed to Spangdahlem AB, Germany, assigned to the 9th Expeditionary Fighter Squadron (EFS) and flew thirty-two combat missions in the former Yugoslavia as part of Operation Allied Force. 786 was flown from Holloman and retired on 11 April 2008 as part of the sixth group of 117s to be retired.

786 seen here in October 1991 (Ben Knowles Photo)

786 marked as the 9th FS commanders aircraft photographed in September 2001. (David F. Brown Photo)

786 is seen here at **NAS Pt. Mugu** on 20 April 2002 with the "Let's Roll" emblem on the nose. (Craig Kaston Photo)

786 in its hangar at Holloman 15 October 2007. (Don Logan Photo)

786 on takeoff at Holloman 14 October 2007. (Don Logan Photo)

786 touching down at Holloman 14 October 2007. (Don Logan Photo)

787 – 80-0787

787 first flew on 20 July 1982 and was accepted by the Air Force 23 August 1982. It was the first aircraft delivered to 4450th TG. It was also the first IOT& E/FOT&E aircraft. (Initial Operational Test and Evaluation, and Follow-on Operational Test and Evaluation respectively) Testing of new concepts was done at the IOT&E level in a test flight setting. If a modification was approved, it would then be tested at the FOT&E level in an operational setting. After both testing phases, the improvement would be incorporated into the USAF fleet. Pete Barnes was assigned to fly IOT&E in #787. The night before Barnes, the second operational TAC F-117A pilot (Bandit #110), made his first flight, Brad Brown (a painter for LADC) painted a dragon design on the side of the aircraft, after hours, on his own time. The aircraft became known as "Pete's Dragon".

Pete's Dragon also had its own patch – a black shield with a green dragon and "Pete's Dragon" in red. Patrick Allen Blazek writes that the origin of the "Pete's Dragon" patch in part derives from the Walt Disney movie of the same name that featured an invisible dragon.

787 was flown from Holloman and retired on 12 October 2007 as part of the second group of 117s to be retired.

787 taxing for out takeoff at Holloman as part of the Silver Stealth Celebration on 27 October 2006. (Don Logan Photo)

787 with 37th TFW markings in September 1991. (Jerry Geer Photo)

787 taking off to take part in the Silver Stealth Celebration on 27 October 2006. (Don Logan Photo)

787 on takeoff roll 19 July 2004 at RIAT Fairford. (Pete Snowdon Photo)

787 on approach returning from the Silver Stealth fly-by on 27 October 2006. (Don Logan Photo)

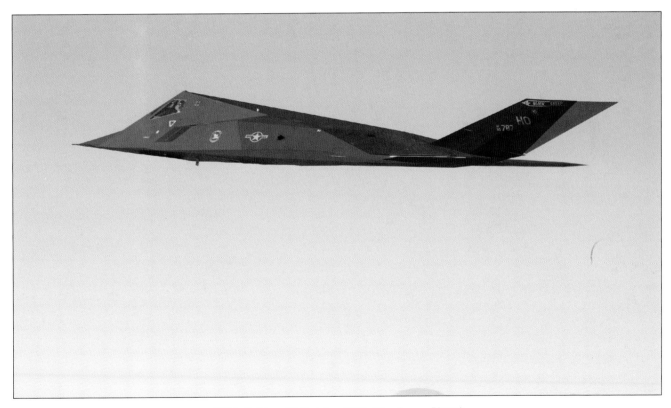

787 inflight on 27 October 2006. (Don Logan Photo)

788 – 80-0788

First flight was on 8 September 1982. It was accepted by the Air Force 22 October 1982. On 21 February 1999 788, then assigned to the 7th FS deployed to Aviano AB, Italy, assigned to the 8th Expeditionary Fighter Squadron (EFS) and flew forty-four combat missions in the former Yugoslavia as part of Operation Allied Force. 788 was flown from Holloman and retired on 11 April 2008 as part of the sixth group of 117s to be retired.

788 marked as a 7th FS Screamin Demons jet on 21 March 1998. (Norris Graser Photo)

789 – 80-0789

BLACK MAGIC First flight 27 October 1982, Accepted by the Air Force 17 November 1982. During Desert Storm 789 flew thirty-one combat missions as part of the 416 TFS, and flew nine combat missions during Operation Iraqi Freedom. It was part of first group retired to Tonopah for storage on 13 March 2007.

789 at Edwards AFB with 37th TFW markings on 6 October 1990.

789 ... of the Silver Stealth Celebration on 27 October 2006. (Don Logan Photo)

... Holloman on 11 August 2006. (Don Logan Photo)

789 on touch down returning from the Silver Stealth fly-by on 27 October 2006. (Don Logan Photo)

LOCKHEED F-117 NIGHT HAWKS

790 – 80-0790

DEADLY JESTER First flight 11 November 1982, Accepted by the Air Force 11 December 1982, Delivered to 4450th TG in Tonopah in December 1982 after trials at Groom Lake. It was used for public unveiling ceremony at Nellis AFB, April 1990. In June 1990 790 was one of six jets that deployed to England AFB, Louisiana and had a Sharkmouth applied to the aircraft.

During Desert Storm 790 flew thirty combat missions while assigned to the 415th TFS. 790 suffered the most 'serious' damage of the Gulf War when it blew a nose wheel on landing. 790 was part of first group retired to Tonopah for storage on 13 March 2007.

790 at Nellis on 21 April 1990 marked as the 415th TFS/AMU Flagship (above and below). (Marty Isham Photo)

(Marty Isham Photo)

790 with 37th FW markings in on 11 October 1991. (Keith Snyder Photo)

In June 1990 790 was one of the F-117 deployed to England AFB, Louisiana home of the A-10s of the 23rd TFW Flying Tigers. The F-117 were adorned with cardboard shark mouths in tribute to the Flying Tigers of the 23rd TFW.

790 enters the last chance arming at the end of the runway for an early morning takeoff at Holloman on 9th August 2006. (Don Logan Photo)

791 – 80-0791

LAZY ACE First flight 22 November 1982, Accepted by the Air Force 13 December 1982, Delivered to 4450th TG in Tonopah in December 1982 after trials at Groom Lake. 791 while assigned to the 415th TFS 33 Desert Storm combat missions. On 21 February 1999 791, then assigned to the 7th FS deployed to Aviano AB, Italy, assigned to the 8th Expeditionary Fighter Squadron (EFS) and flew thirty-seven combat missions in the former Yugoslavia as part of Operation Allied Force. 791 was flown from Holloman and retired on 25 January 2008 as part of the third group of 117s to be retired.

791 with Desert Storm Mission markings at Nellis on 21 April 1990. (Marty Isham Photo)

791 at McConnell AFB, Kansas on 18 September 1992 marked as the 417th FS Flagship. (Don Logan Photo)

791 on approach returning from the Silver Stealth fly-by on 27 October 2006. (Don Logan Photo)

791 taxis out for takeoff at Holloman on 14 October 2007. (Don Logan Photo)

791 touching down at Holloman 14 October 2007. (Don Logan Photo)

791 as the landing gear retracts on takeoff. (Don Logan Photo)

791 at Kunsan AB, Korea on 21 March 2007. (USAF)

791 taxis out for an evening launch at Holloman on 15 October 2007. (Don Logan Photo)

PRODUCTION LOT 3 NIGHT HAWKS

792 – 80-0792

792 first flew on 9 December 1982 and was accepted by the Air Force on 22 December 1982, Delivered to 4450th TG in Tonopah in December 1982 after trials at Groom Lake.

792 crashed 11 July 1986 as a result of Spatial Disorientation. The pilot Major Ross E. Mulhare was killed in the crash. (No photos are available of this aircraft.)

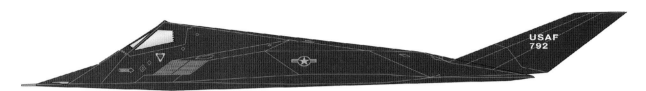

(Jack Morris JDMC Aviation Graphics)

793 – 81-10793

793 first flew on 20 January 1983 and was accepted by the Air Force on 1 February 1983, During Desert Storm 793 flew thirty-three combat missions. 793 flew thirty-seven combat missions in the former Yugoslavia as part of Operation Allied Force. It crashed at Martin State Airport, Baltimore, Maryland on 14 September 1997 during Air show fly by due to missing wing bolts. The pilot ejected safely.

793 in the hangar at Tonopah. (USAF)

793 in the hardened shelter at Khamis Mushair, Saudi Arabia prior to a Desert Storm Mission. (USAF)

On 13 September 1997 crashed near Glen Martin State Airport, Middle River, Maryland. Photos 1 thru 4 show the inflight break-up of the aircraft prior to the crash. (All four Stan Piet Photos)

#1

#2

#3

#4

794 – 81-10794

DELTA DAWN first flew on 4 March 1983 and was accepted by the Air Force on 15 April 1983. During Desert Storm 794 flew thirty-five combat missions while assigned to the 415th TFS. On 4 April 1999 794, then assigned to the 9th FS deployed to Spangdahlem AB, Germany, assigned to the 9th Expeditionary Fighter Squadron (EFS) and flew twenty-nine combat missions in the former Yugoslavia as part of Operation Allied Force and eight combat missions as part of Operation Iraqi Freedom. 794 was flown from Holloman and retired on 12 October 2007 as part of the second group of 117s to be retired.

794 rolls out after touch down following a Red Flag mission at Nellis AFB on 13 February 2007. (Don Logan Photo)

794 on the ramp awaiting takeoff at Holloman as part of the Silver Stealth Celebration on 27 October 2006. (Don Logan Photo)

794 on takeoff at Holloman as part of the Silver Stealth Celebration on 27 October 2006. (Don Logan Photo)

794 taxing for out takeoff at Holloman. (Don Logan Photo)

795 – 81-10795

795's first flight occurred on 7 June 1983. It was accepted by the Air Force 9 September 1983. On 21 February 1999 795, then assigned to the 8th FS deployed to Aviano AB, Italy, assigned to the 8th Expeditionary Fighter Squadron (EFS) and flew thirty-one combat missions in the former Yugoslavia as part of Operation Allied Force. 795 was part of first group retired to Tonopah for storage on 13 March 2007.

795 enters the last chance arming at the end of the runway for an early morning takeoff at Holloman on 9th August 2006. (Don Logan Photo)

795 over the end of the runway for landing at Holloman on 10 August 2006. (Don Logan Photo)

795 touching down at Holloman on 10 August 2006. (Don Logan Photo)

795 on takeoff at Holloman as part of the Silver Stealth Celebration on 27 October 2006. (Don Logan Photo)

796 – 81-10796

FATAL ATTRACTION first flew on 16 June 1983 and was accepted by the Air Force on 4 August 1983. During Desert Storm 796 flew twenty-nine combat missions while assigned to the 415th TFS. 796 was flown from Holloman and retired on 25 January 2008 as part of the third group of 117s to be retired.

796 in flight with early 37th TFW markings. (Lockheed Martin Aeronautics Company)

796 in flight marked as the 49th OG (Operations Group) Flagship over White Sands, New Mexico. (Lockheed Martin Aeronautics Company)

796 at Holloman on 9 October 1995. (Norman E. Taylor)

796 as the landing gear retracts on takeoff on 27 October 2006. (Don Logan Photo)

796 taxing for out takeoff at Holloman on 15 October 2007. (Don Logan Photo)

796 taxing off the runway after landing at Holloman on 15 October 2007. (Don Logan Photo)

796 taxis out for an evening launch at Holloman on 15 October 2007. (Don Logan Photo)

797 – 81-10797

SPELL BOUND first flew on 3 August 1983 and was accepted by the Air Force on 31 August 1983. During Desert Storm 797 flew eight combat missions while assigned to the 416th TFS. At the end of its career it was marked as the 7th Fighter Squadron flagship. 797 was flown from Holloman and retired on 12 October 2007 as part of the second group of 117s to be retired.

797 at Volk Field, Wisconsin on 13 July 2001. (Nate Leong Photo)

The ground crew prepares 797 for a Red Flag mission at Nellis AFB. (USAF)

797 taxis back following a local area mission at Holloman on 8 August 2006. (Don Logan Photo)

797 on takeoff at Holloman as part of the Silver Stealth Celebration on 27 October 2006. (Don Logan Photo)

798 – 81-10798

ACES AND EIGHTS first flew on 25 August 1983 and was accepted by the Air Force on 3 October 1983. During Desert Storm 798 flew thirty-four combat missions while assigned to the 415th TFS. At the end of its career it was marked as the 49th Fighter Wing flagship. 798 was flown from Holloman and retired on 12 October 2007 as part of the second group of 117s to be retired.

Marked as the 49th FW Flagship 798 takes off at Holloman as part of the Silver Stealth Celebration on 27 October 2006. (Don Logan Photo)

The 49th FW Flagship, 798, taxis out for take off at Holloman. (Don Logan Photo)

PRODUCTION LOT 4 NIGHT HAWKS

799 – 82-0799

MIDNIGHT RIDER's first flight occurred on 22 September 1983. It was accepted by the Air Force on 28 October 1983. It was delivered to 4450th TG on the same day enabling the group to attain IOC (Initial Operational Capability). 799 has a total of fifty-four combat missions, twenty-one during Desert Storm while assigned to the 416th TFS, twenty-two combat missions in the former Yugoslavia while assigned to the 9th Expeditionary Fighter Squadron (EFS) as part of Operation Allied Force, and eleven combat missions during Iraqi Freedom (OIF), the most OIF missions flown by an F-117. 799 was flown from Holloman and retired on 31 January 2008 as part of the fifth group of 117s to be retired.

799 is seen here at Holloman AFB in December 1997. (Keith Snyder Photo)

799 over the end of the runway for landing at Holloman on 15 October 2007. (Don Logan Photo)

799 on takeoff at Holloman on 15 October 2007. (Don Logan Photo)

799 taxing out at Holloman on 14 October 2007. (Don Logan Photo)

799 at touch down on 15 October 2007. (Don Logan Photo)

799 jettisoning its drag chute after landing at Holloman on 15 October 2007. (Don Logan Photo)

799 taxing off the runway on 15 October 2007. (Don Logan Photo)

800 – 82-0800

BLACK SHEEP I first flew on 10 November 1983 and was accepted by the Air Force on 7 December 1983. On 21 February 1999 800, then assigned to the 8th FS deployed to Aviano AB, Italy, assigned to the 8th Expeditionary Fighter Squadron (EFS) and flew thirty-eight combat missions in the former Yugoslavia as part of Operation Allied Force, and five combat missions during Iraqi Freedom. At the end of its career it was marked as the 8th Fighter Squadron flagship. 800 was flown from Holloman and retired on 22 April 2007 as part of the last (seventh) group of 117s to be retired.

800 at Holloman in April 1994. (Ben Knowles Photo)

Marked as the 8th FS Flagship, 800 taxing out at Holloman on 27 October 2006. (Don Logan Photo)

The 8th FS Flagship, 82-0800 is seen here in the final turn, landing at Nellis. (Dr. Séan Wilson Prime Images Photo)

800 over the end of the runway for landing at Holloman on 27 October 2006. (Don Logan Photo)

800 still marked as the 8th FS Flagship overhead at Palmdale on its retirement flight 22 April 2008. (Damon J. Duran Photo)

801 – 82-0801

PERPETRATOR first flew on 21 December 1983 and was accepted by the Air Force on 15 February 1984. During Desert Storm PERPETRATOR flew thirty-eight combat missions while assigned to the 415th TFS. 801 crashed 4 August 1992 approximately eight miles northeast of Holloman AFB due to improper installation of a bleed air duct. The pilot Captain John B. Mills, 416th FS, ejected safely. (No photos of this aircraft are available.)

(Jack Morris JDMC Aviation Graphics)

802 – 82-0802

BLACK MAGIC's first flight occurred on 7 March 1984. It was accepted by the Air Force on 6 April 1984. 802 flew nineteen combat missions during Desert Storm while assigned to the 416th TFS. 802 was flown from Holloman and retired on 12 October 2007 as part of the second group of 117s to be retired.

802 in flight with early 37th TFW markings. (Lockheed Martin Aeronautics Company)

802 over Half Dome, Yosemite National Park, California. (Lockheed Martin Aeronautics Company)

802 enters the last chance arming at the end of the runway for an early morning takeoff at Holloman on 9 August 2006. (Don Logan Photo)

803 – 82-0803

UNEXPECTED GUEST first flew on 8 May 1984 and was accepted by the Air Force on 22 June 1984. Starting on 19 December 1989 803 flew combat missions in Panama as part of Operation Just Cause. During Desert Storm 803 while assigned to the 416th TFS flew thirty-three combat missions. On 21 February 1999 803, then assigned to the 8th FS deployed to Aviano AB, Italy, assigned to the 8th Expeditionary Fighter Squadron (EFS) and flew forty-four combat missions in the former Yugoslavia as part of Operation Allied Force. 803 has the greatest total number of combat missions of any F-117. In early 2007 803 was flown to Palmdale and retired on 23 March 2007.

803 Marked as the 49th FW Flagship at Shaw AFB, N.C. on 27 April 1996. (Norman E. Taylor Photo)

803 rolls out after touch down following a Red Flag mission at Nellis AFB on 13 February 2007. (Don Logan Photo)

803 on takeoff at Holloman on 27 October 2006. (Don Logan Photo)

804 – 82-0804

RAMMER first flew on 25 May 1984 and was accepted by the Air Force on 20 June 1984. It was assigned to Det. 1 57th Wing at Holloman AFB for operational test and evaluation purposes. It was also the 7th FS Flagship. 804 was flown from Holloman and retired on 11 April 2008 as part of the sixth group of 117s to be retired.

804, was part of the Dragon Test Team with a **WA** tail code when photographed in front of the Thunderbird hangar at Nellis (above), and in a hangar at Nellis (below) with an unusual weapons load – a **SUU-20 Practice Bomb Dispenser. (Marty Isham Photos)**

(USAF)

A bottom view of 804 with a WA tail code. (Tony R. Landis Photo)

804 marked as the 7th FS Flagship on 12 May 1995. (Keith Snyder Photo)

805 – 82-0805

805's first flight occurred 5 July 1984. It was accepted by the Air Force 2 August 1984. On 21 February 1999 805, then assigned to the 7th FS deployed to Aviano AB, Italy, assigned to the 8th Expeditionary Fighter Squadron (EFS) and flew fifty combat missions in the former Yugoslavia as part of Operation Allied Force. Fifty combat missions were the most logged by an F-117 in OAF. 805 was flown from Holloman and retired on 12 October 2007 as part of the second group of 117s to be retired.

805 marked as the 9th FS Flagship.

805 on approach for landing at Holloman on 27 October 2006 following the Silver Stealth fly-by. (Don Logan Photo)

805 taxiing out on 27 October 2006 for the Silver Stealth fly-by. (Don Logan Photo)

805 taking off at Holloman on 27 October 2006 for the Silver Stealth fly-by. (Don Logan Photo)

806 – 82-0806

SOMETHING WICKED first flew on 20 August 1984 and was accepted by the Air Force on 12 September 1984, During Desert Storm 806, while assigned to the 415th TFS flew thirty-nine combat missions. On 21 February 1999 806, then assigned to the 7th FS deployed to Aviano AB, Italy, assigned to the 8th Expeditionary Fighter Squadron (EFS) and flew five combat missions in the former Yugoslavia as part of Operation Allied Force (OAF). On March 27th, 1999 during its fifth OAF mission F-117A 806 became the first combat loss of an F-117A. Earlier that evening on the fourth night of OAF, 806 took off from Aviano Air Base, Italy using the call sign "Vega 31". A Russian made SA-3 Neva Surface to Air Missile (SAM) exploded very close to the F-117A at about 8:15 PM local time (2:15 PM EST). The blast caused enough damage to 806 that the aircraft went out of control. The pilot ejected and was recovered by a Combat Search and Rescue (CSAR) Team.

806 marked as the 49th FW Flagship at NAS Whidbey Island on 20 June 1992. Note the multi-color 49th Fighter Wing emblem on the fuselage side. (Frank McCurdy Photo)

806 is seen here on 30 May 1999 with 9th FS markings. (Keith Snyder Photo)

This **USAF** photo of 806 taken after its arrival at Aviano **AB**, Italy is probably the last photo of 806 prior to it being shot down. **(USAF)**

Photos of the wreckage of 806.

PRODUCTION LOT 5 NIGHT HAWKS

807 – 83-0807

807 first flew on 13 September 1984 and was accepted by the Air Force on 28 November 1984. It replaced #787 for FOT&E in early 1985. The Dragon name had now become permanently associated with F117 FOT&E. The USAF personnel involved in the FOT&E program began calling themselves the "Dragon Test Team", and decided that they needed a group patch rather than one associated with a specific aircraft. The first generation Dragon Test Team patch appeared in 1986. The Dragon Test Team members had been under the jurisdiction of the 4450th TG. On 5 October, 1989, (The same day the

4450th TG became the 37th TFW.) TAC activated the Dragon Test Team as Det. 1, 57th Fighter Weapons Wing, at Tonopah Test Range. During Desert Storm 807 flew 14 combat missions while assigned to the 415th TFS. On 21 February 1999 807, then assigned to the 9th FS deployed to Aviano AB, Italy, assigned to the 8th Expeditionary Fighter Squadron (EFS) and flew forty-three combat missions in the former Yugoslavia as part of Operation Allied Force. 807 was flown from Holloman and retired on 11 April 2008 as part of the sixth group of 117s to be retired.

807 on the ramp at Holloman 16 October 2007. (Dr. Séan Wilson Prime Images Photo)

807 seen here with 37th FW unit markings. (Lockheed Martin Aeronautics Company)

807 in 37th FW markings taken at Shaw AFB, South Carolina in May 1992. (Norman E. Taylor Photo)

807 was one of the jets that deployed to Europe in 1993. The photo was taken on 7th July 1993. (Brian C. Rogers Collection)

807 seen here in November 2001. (David F. Brown Photo)

807 taxiing with Drag chute deployed, turning to prepare to jettison the chute on 15 October 2007. (Don Logan Photo)

807 jettisoning the drag chute on 15 October 2007. (Don Logan Photo)

808 – 83-0808

THOR's first flight occurred on 23 October 1984. It was accepted by the Air Force on 21 December 1984. During Desert Storm 808 flew thirty-seven combat missions while assigned to the 415th TFS. 808 was flown from Holloman and retired on 29 January 2008 as part of the fourth group of 117s to be retired.

808 on the ramp at Nellis on 1 April 1991. (Norris Graser Photo)

808 taxiing out for takeoff at Holloman 8 August 2006. (Don Logan Photo)

808 in its hangar at Holloman 15 October 2007. (Don Logan Photo)

809 – 84-0809

First flight occurred on 3 January 1985 and 809 was accepted by the Air Force on 16 April 1985. On 4 April 1999 809 then assigned to the 9th FS deployed to Spangdahlem AB, Germany, assigned to the 9th Expeditionary Fighter Squadron (EFS) and flew 17 combat missions in the former Yugoslavia as part of Operation Allied Force. At the end of its career it was marked as the 9th Fighter Squadron flagship. 809 was flown from Holloman and retired on 22 April 2008 as part of the last (seventh) group of 117s to be retired.

809 marked as the 9th FS Flagship on the Holloman ramp at sundown on 26 October 2006. (Don Logan Photo)

809 marked in 37th FW markings.

809 at Langley AFB, Virginia in October 1992. It was assigned to the East Coast F-117 Demonstration Team at the time. (Don Logan Photo)

809 accelerating for takeoff at Holloman on 10 August 2006. (Don Logan Photo)

809 marked as the 9th FS Flagship on the Holloman ramp on 26 October 2006. (Don Logan Photo)

809 still marked as the 9th FS Flagship overhead at Palmdale on its retirement flight 22 April 2008. (Damon J. Duran Photo)

810 – 84-0810

DARK ANGEL's first flight occurred 18 January 1985 and was accepted by the Air Force on 14 February 1985. During Desert Storm 810 flew twenty-six combat missions while assigned to the 416th TFS. On 4 April 1999 810, then assigned to the 9th FS deployed to Spangdahlem AB, Germany, assigned to the 9th Expeditionary Fighter Squadron (EFS) and flew eighteen combat missions in the former Yugoslavia as part of Operation Allied Force. 810 was flown from Holloman and retired on 25 January 2008 as part of the third group of 117s to be retired.

810 on the ramp at Nellis on 1 April 1991. (Norris Graser Photo)

810 taxiing out on at Holloman on 27 October 2006. for the Silver Stealth fly-by. (Don Logan Photo)

810 at Kunsan AB, Republic of Korea on 21 March 2007. (USAF)

810 taking off at Holloman on 27 October 2006. for the Silver Stealth fly-by. (Don Logan Photo)

PRODUCTION LOT 6 NIGHT HAWKS

811 – 84-0811

DOUBLE DOWN first flew on 8 March 1985 and was accepted by the Air Force 29 March 1985. During Desert Storm 811 flew thirty-three combat missions while assigned to the 415th TFS. At the end of its career 811 was assigned to the 410th TS/412th TW at Palmdale, California flying test missions.

811 in 410th TS markings (above and below). (Lockheed Martin Aeronautics Company by Andy Wolfe)

811 in 410th TS markings (above and below). (Lockheed Martin Aeronautics Company by Andy Wolfe)

811 in 410th TS markings (above and below). Comparing the F-117 with the KC-135 in the above photo shows how large an aircraft the F-117 really is. (Lockheed Martin Aeronautics Company by Andy Wolfe)

812 – 84-0812

AXEL first flew on 1 May 1985 and was accepted by the Air Force on 12 June 1985. During Desert Storm while assigned to the 415th TFS 812 flew forty-two combat missions – the most in Desert Storm by one F-117. For part of its career it was marked as the 49th Operations Group flagship. 812 was flown from Holloman and retired on 29 January 2008 as part of the fourth group of 117s to be retired.

812 seen here at Miramar Naval Air Station on 26 August marked as the 49th OG (Operations Group) Flagship. (Craig Kaston Photo)

Still displaying 49th OG markings 812 is seen here on 31 May 1996. (Tom Kaminski Photo)

812 is seen here with the 7th FS blue tail stripe at Holloman on 27 October 2006. (Don Logan Photo)

812 on the ramp awaiting takeoff at Holloman as part of the Silver Stealth Celebration on 27 October 2006. (Don Logan Photo)

812 just after takeoff for the Silver Stealth Celebration Fly-by on 27 October 2006. (Don Logan Photo)

PRODUCTION LOT 7 NIGHT HAWKS

813 – 85-0813

THE TOXIC AVENGER's first flight occurred on 7 June 1985 and was accepted by the Air Force on 10 July 1985. Starting on 19 December 1989 813 flew combat missions in Panama as part of Operation Just Cause. During Desert Storm 813 flew thirty-five combat missions while assigned to the 416th TFS.

813 was Col. Alton C. (Al) Whitley's (37th TFW Commander) aircraft during Operation Desert Storm. 813 was flown from Holloman and retired on 25 January 2008 as part of the third group of 117s to be retired.

813 on the ramp at Holloman 16 October 2007. just after sundown. (Dr. Séan Wilson Prime Images Photo)

813 on the ramp at Nellis AFB 1 April 1991. (Marty Isham Photo)

813 on the ramp at Nellis AFB 1 April 1991. (Marty Isham Photo)

813 on the ramp at Holloman on 27 October 2006. (Don Logan Photo)

813 over the runway just prior to touch down at Holloman on 27 October 2006, following the Silver Stealth fly-by. (Don Logan Photo)

814 – 85-0814

814 first flew on 26 July 1985 and was accepted by the Air Force on 5 September 1985. During Desert Storm 814 flew thirty-four combat missions while assigned to the 416th TFS. 814 flew an additional nine combat missions as part of Operation Iraqi Freedom. 814 was flown from Holloman and retired on 11 April 2008 as part of the sixth group of 117s to be retired.

814 on the ramp at Nellis AFB 1 April 1991. (Marty Isham Photo)

814 in 416th FS markings landing at Tonopah. (Lockheed Martin Aeronautics Company)

814 in 416th FS markings.

814 on the runway at Holloman on 10 August 2006. (Don Logan Photo)

815 – 85-0815

815's first flight occurred on 13 September 1985 and was accepted by the Air Force on 31 October 1985. 815 crashed on 14 October 1987 as a result of Spatial Disorientation. The pilot Major Michael C. Stewart was killed in the crash. The aircraft crashed about 100 miles north of Nellis AFB just east of Tonopah. (No photographs of this aircraft are available.)

(Jack Morris JDMC Aviation Graphics)

816 – 85-0816

LONE WOLF's first flight occurred on 30 October 1985. It was accepted by the Air Force on 20 December 1985. Starting on 19 December 1989 816 flew combat missions in Panama as part of Operation Just Cause. During Desert Storm 816 flew thirty-nine combat missions while assigned to the 416th TFS and for a time it was the 416th squadron flagship. 816

flew an additional eight combat missions as part of Operation Iraqi Freedom. For part of its career it was marked as the 7th Fighter Squadron flagship. 816 was flown from Holloman and retired on 12 October 2007 as part of the second group of 117s to be retired.

816 marked as the 7th FS Flagship over White Sands. (Lockheed Martin Aeronautics Company)

816 marked as a 7th FS Screamin Demon at Langley AFB on 20 September 1994. (Brian C. Rogers Photo)

816 marked as the 7th FS Flagship over White Sands. (Lockheed Martin Aeronautics Company)

816 marked as the 7th FS Flagship on the Nellis AFB flight line.

816 landing at Holloman on 10 August 2006. (Don Logan Photo)

816 taxiing into the arming area at Holloman for a 9 August 2006. local mission. (Don Logan Photo)

816 in the arming area at Holloman on 9 August 2006. (Don Logan Photo)

817 – 85-0817

817s first flew on 9 January 1986 and was accepted by the Air Force on 28 February 1986. Starting on 19 December 1989 817 flew combat missions in Panama as part of Operation Just Cause. During Desert Storm 817 flew eighteen combat missions while assigned to the 416th TFS. On 21 February 1999 817, then assigned to the 8th FS deployed to Aviano AB, Italy, assigned to the 8th Expeditionary Fighter Squadron (FFS) and flew forty combat missions in the former Yugoslavia as part of Operation Allied Force. 817 was part of the first group of F-117s retired to Tonopah for storage on 13 March 2007.

817 taxiing into the arming area at Holloman for a 9 August 2006 local mission (above and below). (Don Logan Photos)

817 on takeoff roll at Holloman for a 10 August 2006. (Don Logan Photo)

818 – 85-0818

THE OVERACHIEVER First flight 11 February 1986, Accepted by the Air Force 22 May 1986. Starting on 19 December 1989 818 flew combat missions in Panama as part of Operation Just Cause. During Desert Storm 818 flew thirty-eight combat missions while assigned to the 415th TFS, and flew twelve combat missions in the former Yugoslavia as part of Operation Allied Force while assigned to the 9th Expeditionary Fighter Squadron (EFS). 818 flew an additional nine combat missions as part of Operation Iraqi Freedom. 818 was retired from Palmdale on 22 June 2007.

818 on the ramp at Nellis AFB.

818 on takeoff (above) and landing (below) at Holloman on 27 October 2006. (Don Logan Photo)

(Don Logan Photo)

819 – 85-0819

RAVEN BEAUTY's first flight occurred on 14 April 1986. It was accepted by the Air Force on 30 April 1986. During Desert Storm 819 flew thirty combat missions as part of the 416th TFS and twenty combat missions in the former Yugoslavia as part of Operation Allied Force. 819 flew an additional five combat missions as part of Operation Iraqi Freedom. 819 was flown from Holloman and retired on 12 October 2007 as part of the second group of 117s to be retired.

819 in 49th FW markings on the ramp at RAF Mildenhall on 25 May 1997. (Peter Greengrass Photo)

819 releasing an inert GBU-12 over the White Sands Bombing range on 9th August 2006. (Don Logan Photo)

Bottom view of 819 from a chase T-38 during flight on 9 August 2006. (Don Logan Photo)

819 landing at Holloman on 10 August 2006. (Don Logan Photo)

819 in the final turn for landing at Holloman AFB from a chase T-38 during flight on 9 August 2006. (Don Logan Photo)

819 in the mountains northeast of Holloman near Sierra Blanca on 9 August 2006. (Don Logan Photo)

PRODUCTION LOT 8 NIGHT HAWKS

820 – 85-0820

820 first flew on 2 May 1986 and was accepted by the Air Force on 19 June 1986, On 21 February 1999 820, then assigned to the 9th FS deployed to Aviano AB, Italy, assigned to the 8th Expeditionary Fighter Squadron (EFS) and flew thirty-seven combat missions in the former Yugoslavia as part of Operation Allied Force. 820 was retired from Palmdale on 23 March 2007.

820 on the ramp at Shaw AFB on 1 August 1998. (Norman E. Taylor Photo)

820 taxiing back from a local area mission at Holloman on 8 August 2006. (Don Logan Photo)

821 – 86-0821

SNEAK ATTACK's first flight occurred on 20 June 1986. It was accepted by the Air Force on 1 August 1986. During Desert Storm 821 flew thirty-two combat missions while assigned to the 415th TFS. On 4 April 1999 821, then assigned to the 9th FS deployed to Spangdahlem AB, Germany, assigned to the 9th Expeditionary Fighter Squadron (EFS) and flew nineteen combat missions in the former Yugoslavia as part of Operation Allied Force. 821 was flown from Holloman and retired on 31 January 2008 as part of the fifth group of 117s to be retired.

821 in 37th FW markings in the Thunderbird Hangar at Nellis. (USAF)

821 in July 1997. (Norris Graser Photo)

821 on approach for landing at Holloman on 27 October 2006. following the Silver Stealth fly-by. (Don Logan Photo)

821 releasing a GBU-27 over the Utah Test and Training Range. (USAF)

821 on the ramp at Holloman on 27 October 2006. awaiting takeoff for the Silver Stealth fly-by. (Don Logan Photo)

822 – 86-0822

822 first flew on 18 August 1986 and was accepted by the Air Force on 18 September 1986. The aircraft crashed on 10 May 1995 as a result of Spatial Disorientation following an autopilot failure. The pilot Captain Kenneth Levens was killed in the crash. The aircraft impacted the ground approximately seven miles south on Zuni, New Mexico on the Zuni Indian Reservation.

822 on 13 August 1994. (Norris Graser Photo)

822 in June 1992. (Norris Graser Photo)

822 on 30 October 1993 at March AFB. (Craig Kaston Photo)

823 – 86-0823

823 first flew on 7 October 1986 and was accepted by the Air Force on 4 December 1986. 823 was flown from Holloman and retired on 12 October 2007 as part of the second group of 117s to be retired.

823 at Langley on 2 June 1995. (Brian C. Rogers Photo)

823 on 18 June 1995. (Randy Walker Photo)

823 just after takeoff for the Silver Stealth Celebration fly-by on 27 October 2006. (Don Logan Photo)

824 – 84-0824

The first flight occurred on 13 November 1986 and was accepted by the Air Force 17 December 1986. During the period July 1991 through January 1992 824 underwent Climatic Testing in the Climatic Test Chamber at Eglin AFB, Florida. On April 5, 1995 824 received major damage due to an engine fuel fire and explosion during a landing at Holloman AFB. The aircraft was repaired and returned to service. 786 flew twenty-seven combat missions in the former Yugoslavia as part of Operation Allied Force and an additional six combat missions during Iraqi Freedom. At the end of its career it was marked as the 49th Operations Group flagship. 824 was flown from Holloman and retired on 22 April 2008 as part of the last (seventh) group of 117s to be retired.

824 marked as the 49th OG Flagship flying with 88-0843 north of Holloman during a flight in March 2008. (Richard Cooper Photo)

824 in 37th TFW markings on 13 October 1990. (Bob Leavitt Photo)

After acknowledgement of the existence of the F-117A program in November 1988. a decision was made to subject it to climatic testing to determine how the aircraft and its systems would perform if it were required to be operated and maintained outside of its normal hangar sheltered environment. Testing began under cold weather conditions (-40 F ambient) on 15 July 1991. (Lockheed Martin Aeronautics Company)

Testing continued through conditions of snow loading, blowing snow, hail, freezing rain, ice and fog, hot weather, water intrusion testing, and concluded in January 1992 with tropical rain and human factors evaluations. 824 was inspected, pre-flighted, and returned to home base shortly thereafter. (Lockheed Martin Aeronautics Company)

(Lockheed Martin Aeronautics Company)

824 being subjected to the hot weather (140 F ambient) testing. (Lockheed Martin Aeronautics Company)

On April 5, 1995 824 received major damage due to an engine fuel fire and explosion during a landing at Holloman AFB. The aircraft was repaired and returned to service. At Palmdale 824's forward fuselage is being lowered onto the fuselage tool for repair following the 5 April 1995 incident. (Lockheed Martin Aeronautics Company)

824 on 14 May 1993. (Norris Graser Photo)

824 at Langley. (Brian C. Rogers Photo)

824 on 16 April 2003 taxiing to the hangars with Operation Iraqi Freedom Mission markings on its return from the deployment. (Lockheed Martin Aeronautics Company)

824 in the hangar at Patterson Field on 11 March 2008 visiting Wright-Patterson AFB as part of the F-117 retirement festivities. (USAF)

824 on the ramp in the "Canyon" at Holloman 17 October 2007. (Dr. Séan Wilson Prime Images Photo)

824 marked as the 49th OG Flagship over White Sands in March 2008. (Richard Cooper Photo)

824 still marked as the 49th OG Flagship overhead at Palmdale on its retirement flight 22 April 2008. (Damon J. Duran Photo)

825 – 84-0825

MAD MAX first flew on 29 January 1987 and was accepted by the Air Force on 25 March 1987. During Desert Storm 825 flew thirty-three combat missions while assigned to the 415th TFS and an additional six combat missions during Iraqi Freedom. 825 was flown from Holloman and retired on 12 October 2007 as part of the second group of 117s to be retired.

825 on the ramp at Nellis AFB on 1 April 1991. (Norris Graser Photo)

825 just prior to touch down at Holloman on 10 August 2006. (Don Logan Photo)

825 on takeoff at RIAT 2007 at RAF Fairford, England on 13 July 2007. (Don Logan Photo)

826 – 84-0826

826's first flight occurred on 2 March 1987. It was accepted by the Air Force 25 March 1987. During Desert Storm it flew twenty-nine combat missions while assigned to the 415th TFS. 826 flew thirty-one combat missions in the former Yugoslavia as part of Operation Allied Force. 826 was flown from Holloman and retired on 29 January 2008 as part of the fourth group of 117s to be retired.

826 Taxiing on to the runway for takeoff at Holloman on 10 August 2006. (Don Logan Photo)

826 at takeoff for the Silver Stealth Celebration fly-by on 27 October 2006. (Don Logan Photo)

826 at touch down At Holloman on 10 August 2006. (Don Logan Photo)

827 – 84-0827

827 first flew on 7 April 1987 and was accepted by the Air Force on 18 May 1987. 827 was flown from Holloman and retired on 12 October 2007 as part of the second group of 117s to be retired.

827 in front of some of the hangars built at Tonopah for the F-117. (Lockheed Martin Aeronautics Company)

827 marked as the 49th FW Flagship on 5 July 1992. (Brian C. Rogers Photo)

827 at NAS Whidbey Island, Washington on 17 July 1993. (Don Abrahamson Photo)

828 – 84-0828

828's first flight occurred on 15 May 1987. It was accepted by the Air Force on 17 June 1987. It was the first F-117 seen by the public at the unveiling at Nellis, 21 April 1990. It wore marking for Colonel Tony Tolin and carrying 37th TFW tail markings. 828 flew thirty-three combat missions in the former Yugoslavia as part of Operation Allied Force. In early 2008 828 was flown from Holloman to Palmdale and became part of the F-117 Combined Test Force (CTF). 828 was retired with the inactivation of the 410th Test Squadron on 1 august 2008.

828 being prepared for flight inside its hangar at Tonopah. (Lockheed Martin Aeronautics Company)

828 on the ramp at Nellis AFB in 37th TFW markings on 21 April 1990. (Craig Kaston Photo)

828 at Langley on 23 June 1993. (Brian C. Rogers Photo)

828 marked as the 49th FW Flagship on 5 July 1992. (Brian C. Rogers Photo)

828 at touch down at Holloman on 14 October 2007. A replacement skin panel is visible just aft of the intake.
It hasn't has the RAM (Radar Absorbent Material) applied yet. (Don Logan Photo)

PRODUCTION LOT 9 NIGHT HAWKS

829 – 85-0829

AVENGING ANGEL first flew on 10 July 1987 and was accepted by the Air Force 27 November 1987. During Desert Storm 829 flew twenty-three combat missions while assigned to the 416th TFS. 829 was retired from Palmdale on 22 June 2007.

829 At McConnell AFB, Kansas for an air show on 20 June 2001 (above and middle). (Don Logan Photo)

(Don Logan Photo)

829 at takeoff for the Silver Stealth Celebration fly-by on 27 October 2006. (Don Logan Photo)

830 – 85-0830

BLACK ASSASSIN's first flight occurred on 3 September 1987, and was accepted by the Air Force 27 November 1987. During Desert Storm 830 flew thirty-one combat missions while assigned to the 416 TFS. It was the first F-117 on public display outside the USA, first at the Paris Air Show in June 1991, and then in the United Kingdom as TR (37th FW) at Mildenhall Air Fete 1992. 830 was flown from Holloman and retired on 25 January 2008 as part of the third group of 117s to be retired.

830 on the ramp at Lockheed's Palmdale facility. It is marked with the Skunk logos behind the cockpit and on the top of the tails. (Lockheed Martin Aeronautics Company)

830 taxiing to the ramp at Nellis AFB on 1 April 1991. (Marty Isham Photo)

830 At McConnell AFB, Kansas for an air show in August 1991. (Don Logan Photo)

830 marked as the 416th TFS/AMU Flagship on 5 October 1990. (Ray Leader Photo)

830 in 49th FW markings at Robbins AFB air show 3 July 1992. (Norman E. Taylor Photo)

(Don Logan Collection Photo)

830 on the runway at Holloman on 10 August 2006. (Don Logan Photo)

830 just prior to touch down at Holloman on 14 October 2007. (Don Logan Photo)

830 on a local area mission at Holloman on 28 August 2006. (Jim Haseltine Photo)

830 and the Gray Dragon 835 performing a formation takeoff as seen from the T-38 chase aircraft on 28 August 2006. (Jim Haseltine Photo)

831 – 86-0831

831 first flew on 20 October 1987 and was accepted by the Air Force on 27 November 1987. It continued to fly from Palmdale with the Combined Test Force for the remainder of its career. 831 made the final flight of the F-117 program flying from Palmdale to retirement at Tonopah on 11 August 2008.

831 was painted with the Lockheed Skunk Works logo for the retirement of Skunk Works President Ben Rich on 6 December 1990. The Skunk had been applied between 27 November and 3 December. It was removed immediately after the 6 December flight. (Lockheed Martin Aeronautics Company)

831 on the ramp at Edwards AFB on 18 October 1992. (Craig Kaston Photo)

832 – 85-0832

ONCE BITTEN's first flight occurred on 10 December 1987. It was accepted by the Air Force on 11 February 1988. During Desert Storm 832 flew thirty combat missions while assigned to the 416th TFS. On 4 April 1999 832, then assigned to the 8th FS deployed to Spangdahlem AB, Germany, assigned to the 9th Expeditionary Fighter Squadron (EFS) and flew seventeen combat missions in the former Yugoslavia as part of Operation Allied Force. 832 was part of first group retired to Tonopah for storage on 13 March 2007.

832 with the Tonopah control tower in the background. (Lockheed Martin Aeronautics Company)

832 taxis back to the hangars from a local area mission on 8 August 2006. (Don Logan Photo)

833 – 85-0833

BLACK DEVIL's first flight occurred on 19 February 1988. It was accepted by the Air Force on 25 May 1988. During Desert Storm 833 flew thirty combat missions while assigned to the 416th TFS. On 21 February 1999 833, then marked as the 49th Fighter Wing Commanders aircraft, deployed to Aviano AB, Italy and was assigned to the 8th Expeditionary Fighter Squadron (EFS) flying forty-five combat missions in the former Yugoslavia as part of Operation Allied Force. 833 was flown from Holloman and retired on 11 April 2008 as part of the sixth group of 117s to be retired.

833 having the last chance inspection accomplished prior to takeoff at Holloman on 15 October 2007. (Don Logan Photo)

833 on the runway at Holloman on 10 August 2006. (Don Logan Photo)

833 on the runway at Holloman on 15 October 2007. (Don Logan Photo)

833 taxiing back to the hangars after landing on 15 October 2007. (Don Logan Photo)

834 – 85-0834

834 first flew on 29 April 1988 and was accepted by the Air Force on 25 May 1988. Starting on 19 December 1989 834 flew combat missions in Panama as part of Operation Just Cause. During Desert Storm 834 flew thirty-four combat missions while assigned to the 416th TFS and an additional six combat missions during Iraqi Freedom. 834 was flown from Holloman and retired on 31 January 2008 as part of the fifth group of 117s to be retired.

834 after takeoff for the Silver Stealth Celebration fly-by on 27 October 2006. Note two of his wingmen turning out in front of him. (Don Logan Photo)

834 taxing out for a night Red Flag mission at Nellis AFB on 10 February 2007. (Kevin Jackson Photo)

834 taxing out for a Red Flag mission at Nellis AFB on 14 February 2007. (Don Logan Photo)

834 taxing on to the runway at Nellis AFB on 15 February 2007. (Don Logan Photo)

834 on takeoff at Nellis AFB on 13 February 2007. (Don Logan Photo)

835 – 85-0835

THE DRAGON first flew on 30 June 1988 and was accepted by the Air Force on 15 August 1988. During Desert Storm 835 flew twenty-six combat missions while assigned to the 416th TFS. 835 was part of first group retired to Tonopah for storage on 13 March 2007.

835 in 49th FW markings taxing out for a Red Flag mission at Nellis AFB in November 1995. (David F. Brown Photo)

835 with the 9th FS red tail stripe at touch down at Holloman. (USAF)

835, the Gray Dragon, in the two gray camouflage in May 2004. (USAF)

835 in the two gray camouflage taxiing in the "Canyon" at Holloman. (USAF)

835 in gunship gray paint on a local area mission at Holloman on 27 August 2006. (Jim Haseltine Photo)

835 faces-off with its T-38 chase prior to a morning takeoff at Holloman on 10 August 2006. (Don Logan Photo)

835 just prior to touch down at Holloman on 10 August 2006. (Don Logan Photo)

835 in the mountains northeast of Holloman on 27 August 2006. (Jim Haseltine Photo)

Bottom view of 835 in gunship gray paint. (Jim Haseltine Photo)

836 – 85-0836

CHRISTINE's first flight occurred on 21 September 1988. It was accepted by the Air Force on 19 October 1988. It was marked as the 37th TFW commander's aircraft before being deemed a 'hangar queen' at Tonopah. During Desert Storm 836 flew thirty-nine combat missions while assigned to the 416th TFS. 836 was flown from Holloman and retired on 31 January 2008 as part of the fifth group of 117s to be retired.

836 is being prepared for launch inside its hangar at Tonopah. (Lockheed Martin Aeronautics Company)

836 releasing a live GBU-27 over the Utah Test and Training Range. (USAF)

836 on the ramp at Langley in October 1992. (Don Logan Photo)

836 just after takeoff at Holloman on 27 October 2006. (Don Logan Photo)

836 taxiing for takeoff at Holloman on 27 October 2006. (Don Logan Photo)

836 at touch down at Holloman on 14 October 2007. (Don Logan Photo)

PRODUCTION LOT 10 NIGHT HAWKS

837 – 86-0837

HABU II first flew on 8 December 1988 and was accepted by the Air Force on 22 February 1989. During Desert Storm 837 flew thirty-one combat missions while assigned to the 416th TFS. From 1994 thru 2000 837 was assigned to the Dragon Test Team. By 2002 it was back in operational service with the 19th FW. 837 was flown from Holloman and retired on 31 January 2008 as part of the fifth group of 117s to be retired.

837 with 57 Wing WA tail codes taxing out for a mission at Holloman AFB.

837 with 57 Wing WA tail codes at Nellis AFB on 19 November 1994. (Craig Kaston Photo)

837 in Dragon Test Team markings with **OT** tail codes at NAS Point Mugu on 26 April 1998. (Craig Kaston Photo)

837 in 49th FW markings at Langley on 17 July 1993. (Brian C. Rogers Photo)

837 in blue 7th FS markings is taxiing back to it hangar after a local area mission on 9 August 2006. (Don Logan Photo)

837 just after takeoff on 27 October 2006. with the Holloman control tower in the background. (Don Logan Photo)

837 at touch down on 14 October 2007. (Don Logan Photo)

837 decelerates after landing on 14 October 2007. (Don Logan Photo)

837 has just jettisoned its drag chute after landing on 14 October 2007. (Don Logan Photo)

837 taxiing back after landing on 14 October 2007. (Don Logan Photo)

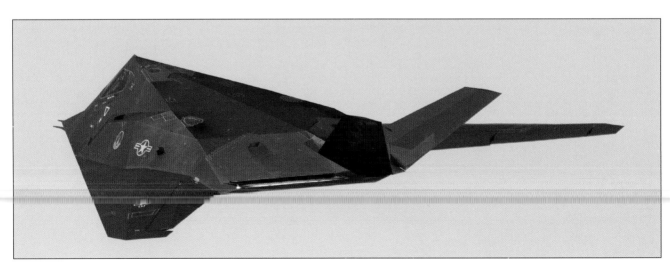

837 climbs out after takeoff on 14 October 2007. (Dr. Séan Wilson Prime Images Photo)

838 – 86-0838

MAGIC HAMMER's first flight occurred on 17 March 1989. It was accepted by the Air Force on 17 May 1989. During Desert Storm 838 flew thirty-six combat missions while assigned to the 416th TFS. 838 was flown from Holloman and retired on 12 October 2007 as part of the second group of 117s to be retired.

838 was marked as 416th TFS Flagship when photographed here in May 1991.

838 in 49th FW markings at Langley on 29 October 1993. (Brian C. Rogers Photo)

838 taxiing into the arming area for a morning flight on 9th October 2006. (Don Logan Photo)

838 taxiing out for a Red Flag mission at Nellis on 14 February 2007. (Don Logan Photo)

838 taxiing onto the runway at Nellis on 14 February 2007. (Don Logan Photo)

838 and his wingman over the Nellis ranges on a Red Flag mission on 12 February 2007. (Dr. Séan Wilson Prime Images Photo)

839 – 86-0839

MIDNIGHT REAPER's first flight occurred on 14 June 1989, and it was accepted by the Air Force on 14 August 1989. During Desert Storm 839 flew thirty-nine combat missions while assigned to the 415th TFS. At the end of Its career It was marked as the 49th Operations Group flagship. 839 was flown from Holloman and retired on 25 January 2008 as part of the third group of 117s to be retired.

839 in early 49th FW markings taking the runway for takeoff.

839 marked as the 49th OG Flagship on the ramp at Holloman at sunset on 26 October 2006. (Don Logan Photo)

839 marked as the 49th OG Flagship on 9th September 2006. (Dr. Séan Wilson Prime Images Photo)

839 over the Nellis ranges on a Red Flag mission on 9th February 2007. (Kevin Jackson Photo)

839 taxiing onto the runway at Nellis on 14 February 2007. (Don Logan Photo)

839 in the parking shelters at Nellis AFB on 10 February 2007. (Kevin Jackson Photo)

839 taxiing out after sunset on 17 October 2007. (Dr. Séan Wilson Prime Images Photo)

840 – 86-0840

BLACK WIDOW first flew on 12 September 1989. It was accepted by the Air Force on 1 November 1989. During Desert Storm 840 flew thirty-two combat missions while assigned to the 416th TFS. 840 was flown from Holloman and retired on 11 April 2008 as part of the sixth group of 117s to be retired.

840 at Langley on 23 June 1993. (Brian C. Rogers Photo)

840 ready to taxi in August 1996. (Jim) Dunn Photo)

840 taxing to the arming area for the Silver Stealth Celebration fly-by on 27 October 2006. (Don Logan Photo)

840 taxiing on to the runway for takeoff at Holloman on 10 August 2006. (Don Logan Photo)

840 on takeoff roll at Nellis for a Red Flag mission on 13 February 2007. (Dr. Séan Wilson Prime Images Photo)

(Lockheed Martin Aeronautics Company)

PRODUCTION LOT 11 NIGHT HAWKS

841 – 88-0841

MYSTIC WARRIOR first flew on 7 December 1989 and was accepted by the Air Force on 8 March 1990. During Desert Storm 841 flew eighteen combat missions while assigned to the 416th TFS. In late 2007 841 was flown from Holloman to Palmdale and was operated as part of the Combined Test Force. 841 was retired with the inactivation of the 410th Flight Test Squadron on 1 August 2008.

841 in early 49th FW markings at Chicago O'Hare International Airport on 27 May 1994. (Norris Graser Photo)

841 at an air show at Altus AFB, Oklahoma on 6 July 1993. (Randy Walker Photo)

841 in the "Canyon" taxing back to its hangar after a local area flight on 8th August 2006. (Don Logan Photo)

841 in 410th TS markings with an ED tail code on approach at Palmdale on 30 October 2007. (Gerhard Plomitzer Photo)

842 – 88-0842

IT'S HAMMERTIME first flew on 13 March 1990 and was accepted by the Air Force on 28 March 1990. During Desert Storm 842 flew thirty-three combat missions while assigned to the 416th TFS. In addition 842 flew twenty-three combat missions in the former Yugoslavia as part of Operation Allied Force and nine combat missions as part of Iraqi Freedom. 842 was flown from Holloman and retired on 29 January 2008 as part of the fourth group of 117s to be retired.

842 in 37th TFW markings.

842 in 8th FS markings with an unusual Black Sheep tail stripe at Shaw AFB on 29 April 1994. (Norman E. Taylor Photo)

842 on 16 April 2003 taxiing to the hangars with Operation Iraqi Freedom Mission markings on its return from the deployment. (Lockheed Martin Aeronautics Company Photo by Denny Lombard)

842 taxing back to its hangar after a local area flight on 8th August 2006. (Don Logan Photo)

842 on the runway for a morning takeoff on 11 August 2006. (Don Logan Photo)

842 just after takeoff for the Silver Stealth fly-by on 27 October 2006. (Don Logan Photo)

843 – 88-0843

AFFECTIONATELY CHRISTINE first flew on 11 May 1990 and was accepted by the Air Force on 12 July 1990. It was the final F-117 aircraft built. During Desert Storm 843 flew thirty-three combat missions while assigned to the 415th TFS. 843 flew twenty-seven combat missions in the former Yugoslavia as part of Operation Allied Force. At the end of its career 843 flew with the U.S. Flag painted on the bottom of the aircraft. It was flown from Holloman and retired on 22 April 2008 as part of the last (seventh) group of 117s to be retired.

The last F-117 843 was formally delivered to the Air Force on 12 July 1990 in a ceremony at Palmdale. (Mick Roth Photo)

843 on the ramp at Nellis AFB on 1 April 1991. (Norris Graser Photo)

843 just after takeoff for the Silver Stealth fly-by on 27 October 2006. (Don Logan Photo)

843 releasing an inert GBU-12. (USAF)

843 taxiing onto the runway at Nellis on 14 February 2007. (Don Logan Photo)

843 taxiing out for a Red Flag mission at Nellis on 14 February 2007. (Don Logan Photo)

843 returning from a Red Flag mission on 12 February 2007. (Dr. Séan Wilson Prime Images Photo)

843 at Patterson Field on 11 March 2008 visiting Wright-Patterson AFB as part of the F-117 retirement festivities. (USAF)

843 marked with the U.S. Flag motif over White Sands in March 2008. (Richard Cooper Photo)

843 overhead at Palmdale on its retirement flight 22 April 2008. (Damon J. Duran Photo)

Companion Aircraft

A-7 COMPANION AIRCRAFT PROGRAM

Due to the restrictions on F-117A flights during the 4450th Tactical Group "black" era, a supplemental aircraft was needed for training and practice and to provide a cover story for the 4450th Test Group's existence.

The aircraft chosen for the job was the Ling-Temco-Vought (LTV) A-7 Corsair II. The A-7 SLUFF (Short Little Ugly Fat Fellow) was chosen because it mirrored the amount of pilot workload expected in the F-117A. In addition it was a single seat aircraft, and since some of the 4450th's pilots had never flown single seat aircraft outside of solo flight in undergraduate pilot flight school it would bring all pilots to a common flight training base line. For example, some of the F-117A pilots had F-4 or F-111 backgrounds. Upon selection to the 4450th, pilots were sent to the Arizona Air National Guard's 162nd TFG at Tucson for pilot conversion into the A-7D.

4450th TG Flagship and wingman over Hoover Dam. (USAF)

In addition to providing an excuse for the 4450th's existence and activities of Avionics Testing, they were also used to maintain pilot currency especially in the early in the program when very few F-117As were available. The pilots learned to fly chase on F-117A test and training flights, perform practice covert deployments, and practice any other purpose that could not be accomplished using F-117As because of the tight security imposed on the F-117A and its operations. Most of the aircraft came from 23rd Tactical Fighter Wing stationed at England AFB, Louisiana. The 23rd TFW was converting to A-10s and the A-7s were programmed to be transferred. There were approximately twenty aircraft, including two of A-7Ks. The 4450th TG was the last active USAF unit to fly the A-7D

A-7 flight operations began in June 1981 concurrent with the very first YF-117A flights. The A-7's wore a unique "LV" tail code (for Las Vegas) and were based officially at Nellis AFB. They were maintained by the 4450th Maintenance Squadron, based at Nellis. Some A-7s operated from Tonopah from the beginning.

A-7s

31 Dec 82	31 May 84	30 Jun 86	31 Aug 88
69-6201	69-6198	69-6200	69-6202
69-6207	69-6201	69-6201	69-6214
69-6244	69-6207	69-6202	69-6225
70-0940	69-6244	69-6207	69-6235
70-0941	70-0940	69-6214	69-6241
70-0969	70-0941	69-6225	69-6244
70-0982	70-0969	69-6235	70-0934
70-1019	70-0982	69-6241	70-0940
70-1020	70-1019	69-6244	70-0941
70-1021	70-1020	70-0940	70-0942
70-1023	70-1021	70-0941	70-0982
70-1051	70-1023	70-0982	70-1005
73-1008 (A-7K)	73-1008 (A-7K)	70-1005	70-1019
79-0469 (A-7K)	79-0469 (A-7K)	70-1019	70-1021
		70-1020	70-1023
		70-1021	74-1760
		70-1023	73-1008 (A-7K)
		74-1760	79-0469 (A-7K)
		73-1008 (A-7K)	
		79-0469 (A-7K)	

69-6235, the 4450th TG Flagship at Nellis AFB. (Marty Isham Photo)

69-6235, the 4450th TG Flagship at Nellis AFB in August 1988. (Marty Isham Photo)

69-6198 at Buckley ANGB, Colorado on 22 December 1984. (Brian C. Rogers Photo)

69-6201 at Davis-Monthan AFB, Arizona on 10 July 1982. (Brian C. Rogers Photo)

69-6207 at Langley AFB on 27 October 1982.

69-6241 at McChord AFB, Washington on 16 September 1986. (Doug Remington Photo)

70-0969 at Davis-Monthan AFB, Arizona on 12 September 1982. (Brian C. Rogers Photo)

70-0982 on 9 August 1987. (Bob Greby Photo)

70-1023 at Williams AFB, Arizona on 18 October 1987. (Douglas Slowiak Photo)

A-7K

The 4450 had two two-seat A-7Ks assigned, 73-1008 and 79-0469. These aircraft were commonly used as support aircraft to gather data during test flights. The Dragon Test Team used the A-7Ks to make sure that test munitions separated cleanly, and to follow the weapon down to impact for spotting purposes.

73-1008 at Davis-Monthan AFB, Arizona on 28 March 1982. 73-1008 was an A-7D modified to the prototype YA-7K, the USAF's first two seat A-7 which first flew in January 1981. (Brian C. Rogers Photo)

73-1008 at Nellis AFB in August 1988. (Marty Isham Photo)

79-0469 at Carswell AFB in 1985. (Brian C. Rogers Photo)

T-38 COMPANION AIRCRAFT PROGRAM

4450th TACTICAL GROUP – 37th TACTICAL FIGHTER WING – 37th FIGHTER WING

60-0572 flying chase with a 37th TFW F-117. (Lockheed Martin Aeronautics Company)

In January 1989, just three months after the USAF admitted the F-117A existed, the elder A-7's were replaced with newer T-38A and AT-38B Talon trainers. Many of these "Talons" formerly belonged to the 4477th TS "Red Eagles" that flew "acquired" Soviet aircraft at Groom Lake, Nevada. One of the AT-38B Talons even served as a USAF Thunderbird before being used in the Red Eagles.

68-8106 is taxiing through the gates between the hangar complex and the runway at Tonopah. (Lockheed Martin Aeronautics Company)

Most of the T-38s were reassigned to training units with the disbanding of the 37th FW:

60-0553	61-0851	65-10350	65-10383
60-0572	61-0870	65-10367	68-8106
61-0848	61-0938	65-10382	

60-0572 marked as the 4450th TG Flagship in June 1982. (Ben Knowles Photo)

60-0553 marked as the 37th TFW Flagship at Nellis in August 1988. (Ben Knowles Photo)

61-0848 in 37th TFW markings at Nellis in September 1991. (Don Logan Collection)

65-10350 marked as the 417th FS Flagship at Shaw AFB on 27 March 1992. (Norman E. Taylor Photo)

61-0851 at Shaw AFB in May 1990. (Norman E. Taylor Photo)

TR T-38 flying chase with a 37th TFW F-117. (Lockheed Martin Aeronautics Company)

49th FIGHTER WING

Prior to the F-117As arrival at Holloman, F-15s and AT-38s were the aircraft of the "Forty Niners". After the F-117As arrival, the Holloman AT-38s were operated by the 417 FS and wore a standard camouflage pattern. This was later changed to a distinctive black paint job after the 417th became the 7th FS. Like the F-117As, originally the AT-38Bs wore just a five-digit number. This was later changed to a small year prefix, three-digit tail number, and a fin flash of three F-117A silhouettes on the tail.

As of 31 Dec 1994 (all T-38A):
64-13175
64-13278
65-10373
65-10376
65-10455
66-8404
67-14831
67-14939
68-8139
68-8141
68-8150
68-8172
68-8177
68-8185
68-8186
68-8204

As of 31 Dec 1999 (all T-38A):
64-13175
65-10373
65-10376
65-10455
67-14831
67-14833
67-14939
68-8139
68-8141
68-8150
68-8172
68-8177
68-8185
68-8186
68-8204

67-14831 in 49th FW markings at Holloman on 21 October 1994. (Craig Kaston Photo)

67-14831 on the runway for takeoff on 10 August 2006. (Don Logan Photo)

67-14833 at Holloman in December 1997. (Keith Snyder Photo)

67-14939 at Langley AFB, Virginia on 1 June 1994. (Brian C. Rogers Photo)

68-8139 with the "Lets Roll" 9-11 emblem on the nose at Holloman on 20 September 2002. (Don Logan Photo)

68-8141 in 49th FW markings at Holloman on 21 October 1994. (Craig Kaston Photo)

68-8150 in the arming area at Holloman awaiting it time for takeoff on 10 August 2006. (Don Logan Photo)

68-8150 with the 8th FS emblem on the intake sits on the ramp at Holloman on 14 October 2007. (Don Logan Photo)

68-8172 with the 7th FS emblem on the intake sits on the ramp at McConnell AFB in October 2003. (Don Logan Photo)

68-8172 with the 8th FS yellow tail stripe taxies back to the ramp at Holloman on 14 October 2007. (Don Logan Photo)

68-8177 with the blue tail stripe of the 7th FS taxis at Holloman for an early morning takeoff on 10 August 2006. (Don Logan Photo)

68-8177 just prior to touchdown at Holloman on 10 August 2006. (Don Logan Photo)

68-8204 at touchdown at Holloman on 15 October 2007. (Don Logan Photo)

Appendices

85-0819 over southeastern New Mexico. (Don Logan Photo)

LOCKHEED F-117 NIGHT HAWKS

INDIVIDUAL F-117 COMBAT MISSIONS

AIRCRAFT NUMBER	JUST CAUSE	DESERT STORM	ALLIED FORCE	IRAQI FREEDOM	TOTAL COMBAT MISSIONS
785		CRASHED – NO COMBAT MISSIONS			
786		24	34		58
787		NO COMBAT MISSIONS			
788			44		44
789		31		9	40
790		30	30		
791		NO COMBAT MISSIONS			
792		CRASHED – NO COMBAT MISSIONS			
793		33	37		70
794		35	29	8	72
795			31		31
796		29			29
797		8			8
798		34			34
799		21	22	11	54
800			38	5	43
801		38			38
802		19			19
803	1	33	44		78
804		NO COMBAT MISSIONS			
805		50			50
806		39	5		44
807		14	43		57
808		37			37
809			17		17
810		26	18		44
811		33			33
812		42			42
813	1	35			36
814		34			34
815		CRASHED – NO COMBAT MISSIONS			
816	1	39		8	48
817	1	18	40		59
818	1	38	12	9	60
819		30	20	5	55
820		37			37
821		32	19		51
822		NO COMBAT MISSIONS			
823		NO COMBAT MISSIONS			
824			27	6	33
825		33		5	38
826		29	31		60
827		NO COMBAT MISSIONS			
828			33		33
829		23			23
830		31			31
831		TEST – NO COMBAT MISSIONS			
832		30	17		47
833		30	45		75
834	1	34		6	41
835		26			26
836		39			39
837		31			31
838		36			36
839		39			39
840		32			32
841		18			18
842		33	23	9	65
843		33	27		60

Cockpit of aircraft 788 photographed at Palmdale, 3 October 2006. (Lockheed Martin Aeronautics Company)

F-117 PROGRAM TAIL CODES

FD	(Y)F-117, F-117 410 TS 412 TW Baja Scorpions Plant 42 – Palmdale, 03/01/93 – 03/10/94
ED	(Y)F-117, F-117 410 FLTS 412 TW Baja Scorpions Plant 42 – Palmdale, 03/10/94 – 08/01/08
HO	F-117 49 FW Fighting Forty-Niners Holloman AFB, 1995 – 04/22/08
HO	F-117 7 FS 49 FW Screamin Demons Holloman AFB, 12/15/93 – 12/15/06
HO	F-117 8 FS 49 FW Black Sheep Holloman AFB, 07/30/93 – 04/22/08
HO	F-117 9 FS 49 FW Iron Knights Holloman AFB, 07/30/93 – 1995
HO	F-117 9 FS 49 FW Flying Knights Holloman AFB, 1995 – 04/22/08
HO	F-117 415 FS 49 FW Nighthawks Holloman AFB, 07/08/92 – 07/30/93
HO	F-117 416 FS 49 FW Knight Riders Holloman AFB, 07/08/92 – 07/30/93
HO	F-117 417 FS 49 FW Bandits Holloman AFB, 07/08/92 – 12/??/93
HO	AT-38B 417 FS 49 FW Bandits Holloman AFB, 07/08/92 – 12/??/93
HO	T-38A 7 CTS 49 FW Screamin Demons Holloman AFB, 06/17/99 – 07/22/05
HO	T-38A 8 FS 49 FW Screamin Demons Holloman AFB, 07/22/05 – 12/15/06
LV	A-7D, A-7K 4450th TG Goatsuckers Nellis AFB
OT	F-117 Det. 1, 79 TEG 53 W Dragon Test Team Holloman AFB, 10/01/96 – late-1998
OT	F-117 Det. 1, 53 TEG 53 W Dragon Test Team Holloman AFB, late-1998 – 10/01/06
TR	F-117 415 TFS 37 TFW Nightstalkers Tonopah TR, 10/05/89 – 10/01/91
TR	F-117 415 FS 37 FW Nightstalkers Tonopah TR, 10/01/91 – late-1992
TR	F-117 415 FS 37 FW Nighthawks Tonopah TR, late-1992 – 07/08/92
TR	F-117 4453 TES 4450 TG Grim Reapers Tonopah TR, 10/01/85 – 10/05/89
TR	F-117 416 TFS 37 TFW Ghostriders Tonopah TR, 10/05/89 – 10/01/91
TR	F-117 416 FS 37 FW Ghostriders Tonopah TR, 10/01/91 – late-1992
TR	F-117 416 FS 37 FW Knight Riders Tonopah TR, late-1992 – 07/30/93
TR	F-117, AT-38B 4451 TS 4450 TG Bandits Tonopah TR, 10/01/85 – 10/05/89
	There were no T-38s or AT-38s assigned to the 4450th TG prior to 1989.
TR	F-117, AT-38B 417 TFTS 37 FW Bandits Tonopah TR, 10/05/89 – 10/01/91
TR	F-117, AT-38B 417 FS 37 FW Bandits Tonopah TR, 10/01/91 – 07/08/92
WA	F-117 Det. 1 57 FWW Dragon Test Team Tonopah TR, 10/05/89 – 10/01/91
WA	F-117 Det. 1 57 FW Dragon Test Team Tonopah TR, 10/01/91 – 06/01/92
WA	F-117 Det. 1 57 FW Dragon Test Team Holloman AFB, 06/01/92 – 02/01/93
WA	F-117 Det. 1 57 W Dragon Test Team Holloman AFB, 02/01/93 – 10/01/95
WA	F-117 Det. 1 53 W Dragon Test Team Holloman AFB, 10/01/95 – 10/01/96